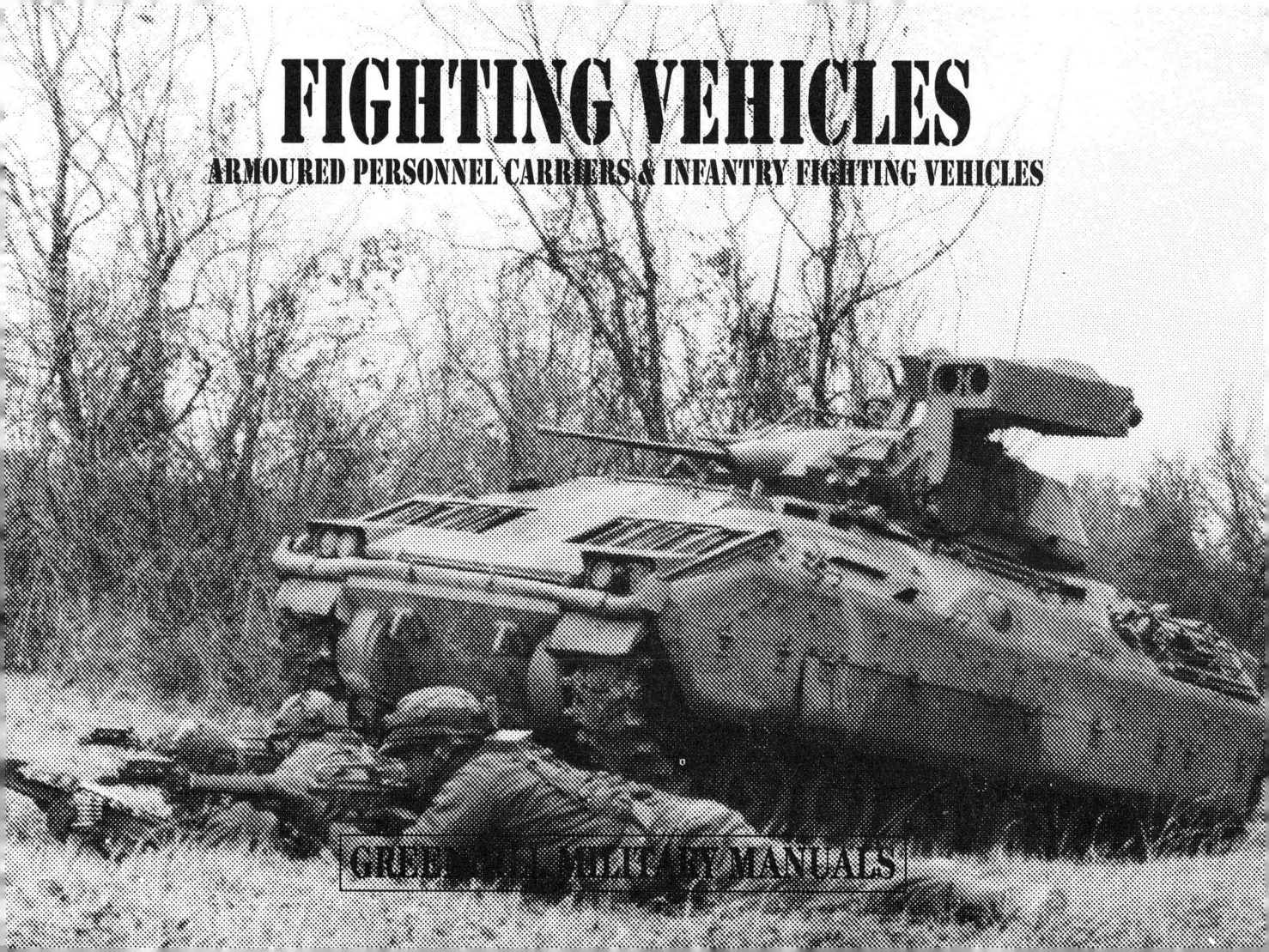

FIGHTING VEHICLES

ARMOURED PERSONNEL CARRIERS & INFANTRY FIGHTING VEHICLES

GREENHILL MILITARY MANUALS

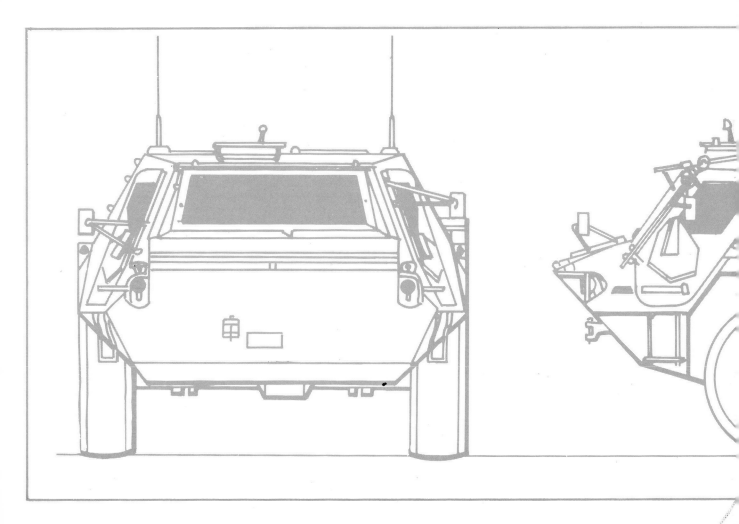

FIGHTING VEHICLES
RMOURED PERSONNEL CARRIERS & INFANTRY FIGHTING VEHICLES

GREENHILL MILITARY MANUALS

T. J. O'MALLEY
ILLUSTRATED BY RAY HUTCHINS

Greenhill Books, London
Stackpole Books, Pennsylvania

Fighting Vehicles: Armoured Personnel Carriers and Infantry Fighting Vehicles
first published 1996 by
Greenhill Books, Lionel Leventhal Limited, Park House
1, Russell Gardens, London NW11 9NN
and
Stackpole Books, 5067 Ritter Road, Mechanicsburg, PA 17055, USA

British Library Cataloguing in Publication Data
O' Malley, T. J..
Fighting Vehicles: Armoured Personnel Carriers and Infantry Fighting Vehicles
- (Greenhill Military Manuals; No. 6)
I. Title II. Hutchins, Ray III. Series 623.7475
ISBN 1-85367-211-4

Library of Congress Cataloging in Publication Data
O' Malley, T. J
Fighting Vehicles: Armoured Personnel Carriers and Infantry Fighting Vehicles
by T. J. O'Malley, illustrated by Ray Hutchins
144p. 15cm - - (Greenhill Military Manuals)
ISBN 1-85367-211-4 (hc)
1. Armored vehicles, Military.   2 Tanks (Military science)
I Title. II. Series.
UG 446.5.O56 1995
358'. 18 - dc20   95 - 15140
CIP

Typeset by Vector Publicity and Communications
Printed and bound in Great Britain by
The Bath Press, Avon

Introduction

Compared to the tank, the armoured personnel carrier (APC) and the infantry fighting vehicle (IFV) have had a brief history. During the Great War a few visionaries had the notion of using armoured vehicles to transport soldiers around the battlefield and the first tanks were able to carry a few infantrymen. But it was not until the 1930s that the writings of armoured warfare prophets Fuller and Liddell Hart led to the first dedicated 'battlefield taxis'.

Both men forecast that future armoured warfare would involve not just tanks but specialised armoured vehicles to transport the support arms upon which the tanks would depend and with whom they would co-operate. The infantry needed something better than their leg-power or road-bound trucks to maintain contact with the mobile armoured spearheads that Liddell Hart and Fuller foresaw.

At first the only nation to absorb their message was Germany, which during the early to mid 1930s was in the throes of a political and social revolution in the aftermath of Hitler coming to power. The concept of what was to become known as 'Blitzkrieg', or Lightning War, followed, based on infantry tactics devised during the Great War. This entailed the use of concentrated offensive power at one point followed by deep and rapid thrusts into the enemy rear, to disrupt and isolate opposing forces. The tank, though ideal for this concept, had to have support.

The result was an array of armoured combat vehicles which covered all aspects of modern warfare from communications to artillery. Among these were infantry half-tracks, a combination of conventional road wheels for steering plus tracks supporting a lightly armoured open body. Such vehicles were complicated and expensive, so relatively few German infantry could be transported like this into battle.

Later came the American M3 half-tracks which were churned out in thousands. The British had their own APCs. In the late 1930s they had small tracked carriers, usually known as Bren Gun or Universal Carriers, but these were more often employed as specialised troop or team transporters rather than as all-purpose APCs, for they could carry only a few troops in an open compartment.

When land battles grew in intensity, the Allies began to use turretless tank chassis as troop carriers to ensure that the infantry could survive. Usually known as Kangaroos, these vehicles were old or obsolete tank chassis with limited carrying capacity.

It was some years after 1945 before the first of what we now recognise as APCs appeared. Initially they were little more than armoured boxes on tracks or wheels. Troops had virtually no view of the outside world and could not use their weapons from within their armoured protection; but were protected against enemy small arms fire and overhead artillery bursts and could thus travel and survive better on the modern battlefield. This generation was typified by the British FV432, the American M59 and (later) the M113.

The Soviet Union was rather late in the APC field. During the Great Patriotic War (as they called the Second World War) Red Army 'tank descent' troops were carried into battle on tank exteriors. After 1945 that procedure was gradually discarded in favour of transport inside a well-designed APC, which became the yardstick that the West would follow.

Contents

The Future

There is no firm line of thought as to which path the next generations of APCs and IFVs might take. There seems to be a general reluctance to follow the usual tank path of 'larger and heavier' for the design limits of the armoured infantry vehicles appear to have been reached. Some IFVs (such as the German Marder 1) already resemble light tanks and certainly weigh as much. To emphasise this point there are already some IFVs being considered as platforms for low recoil 105 mm guns originally intended for mounting on tanks. While such upgrades will remove such heavily-armed vehicles from the IFV category the fact that such an option is available demonstrates how the IFV/APC has grown from a mobile armoured box to a powerful armoured combat vehicle.

No firm preference for tracks over wheels has emerged. Both have established their place on the battlefield. Tracks may provide more mobility but wheels are less complex and expensive and, in general terms, more suited to long range operations. (The South African Ratel, with an operational range of of some 1,000km, is a good example of the latter.)

There seems to be a general acceptance that protection levels will have to increase to counter ever-growing threats that ATGWs and close-in infantry anti-armour weapons can produce but a point will be reached where the weights imposed by thick armoured carapaces will seriously impede performance. However, relatively lightweight non-metallic armours are already in service and further developments in this area are to be expected.

There will almost certainly be firepower enhancements. The current IFV armament calibre bracket is from 20 to 30 mm. As armoured protection increases gun calibres will need to grow accordingly. There are several avenues of thought on this subject. The Swedes have already adopted 40 mm gun as the main armament for their CV 90 IFV while in both France and the UK consideration is being given to a 45 mm gun firing low volume cased telescoped ammunition (CTA) more than capable of destroying any future opposition IFV. For yet another indication of current fire enhancement approaches, the Bradley 25 mm cannon performance has recently been greatly improved by the introduction of more powerful kinetic energy ammunition, delaying any need for weapon replacement for the foreseeable future.

While on this subject, the missile will not completely replace gun armaments for the gun has demonstrated that it can be a far more versatile, economic and effective projectile delivery system than the expensive one-shot guided missile.

It may well emerge that models such as the M2/M3 Bradley, Warrior, Pandur and Piranha will remain the yardsticks of IFV/APC development for some time to come. However, that does not mean that their forms will remain fixed. We are already into the second generation of IFVs which, in general terms, have enhanced performance fire control systems, the option of add-on armour, advanced drive trains and suspensions, and better all-round crew protection (such as engine compartment fire suppression) and high performance communications systems. The latest Bradleys are very different visually and mechanically from the original models.

The IFV is not completely replacing the APC. There is still a requirement for dedicated APCs for many tasks, not the least being for the many support arms who provide specialist teams such as combat engineers, signallers, recovery and repair specialists, medical services and so forth, most of which are covered in this book. For many such roles protected internal space is still more important than external firepower so the APC still has a long future ahead.

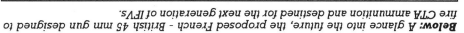

Below: A glance into the future, the proposed French - British 45 mm gun designed to fire CTA ammunition and destined for the next generation of IFVs.

Above: A vision of the future - troops leaving a future French 8 x 8 IFV design armed with a 30 mm cannon.

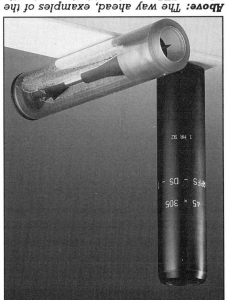

Above: The way ahead, examples of the 45 mm CTA rounds with the projectile totally enclosed within the propellant.

Although allocated under Argentina the **TAMSE VCTP** was originally a German development, the firm of Thyssen having been awarded a 1974 contract by the Argentinian government for the development of a 105 mm gun tank and an IFV using the same basic chassis and hull.

Argentinian development and production of the **VCTP IFV** and its variants was erratic due to the state of the local economy, to the point when production in Argentina was terminated after 350 examples (of all types, including the tank variant) out of a planned 500 plus had been completed.

The basic **VCTP IFV** is essentially similar in layout to the German Marder but simplified and modified to meet Argentinian Army requirements and has a more powerful 720 hp MTU diesel power pack.

The main armament is carried in a two-man power-operated turret armed with a 20 mm Oerlikon cannon and an externally mounted 7.62 mm MG for air and local defence.

A further 7.62 mm MG is located in a remotely-controlled mounting over the hull rear. This MG is controlled from within the troop compartment which can accommodate up to ten soldiers and their personal equipment. The troops enter and leave the vehicle via a door in the hull rear and there are also roof hatches.

Firing ports and vision devices are located around the troop compartment for use by the occupants. Four smoke grenade launchers are mounted each side of the hull. An essentially similar command post variant has provision for only six in the troop compartment and lacks a turret, as does a 120 mm mortar carrier version (the VCTM) which has a crew of five.

An ARV version was produced in prototype form and only two 155 mm self-propelled guns (the VCA) were produced. The VCLC MRL was intended to fire 160 or 350 mm artillery rockets from pre-loaded 'packs' but only prototypes were completed for testing before production ceased.

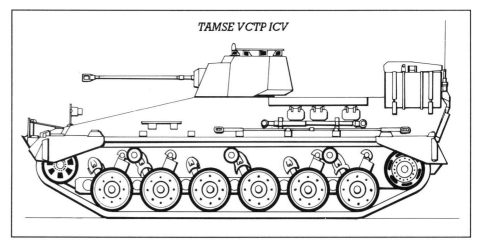

TAMSE VCTP ICV

Specification

Crew: 2
Seating: 10
Weight: (combat) 28,000 kg
Length: 6.83 m
Width: 3.32 m
Height: 2.68 m
Ground clearance: 0.45 m
Track: 2.62 m
Max speed: (road) 80 km/h
Fuel capacity: 640 + 400 litres
Range: 590 + 350 km

Fording: 1.5 m
Vertical obstacle: 1 m
Engine: MTU MB 833 V6 diesel
Power output: 720 hp
Suspension: torsion bar
Armament: 20 mm cannon, 2 x 7.62 mm machine guns
Variants: VCPC command post, VCRT ARV, VCLC MRL, VCTM mortar carrier, VCA self-propelled gun

The VCTP IFV, the Argentinian-built version of the German Marder travelling through heavy mud.

Steyr Pandur   Austria

The Steyr-Daimler-Puch **Pandur** is a 6 x 6 configuration wheeled combat vehicle (6 x 4 on roads) which can only be described as multi-purpose for it was developed to fulfil a wide variety of combat roles, with all variants sharing the same automotive components.

Developed as a private venture, the first example appeared in 1985. Since then a series of pre-production variants have been produced to demonstrate a number of roles, from unarmed ambulance to various turreted models mounting weapons from 12.7 mm MGs to 30 mm cannon.

The base model **Pandur** APC does not have a turret, although firing ports for the occupants' weapons can be provided in the hull sides, while two doors for the passengers are provided at the rear; there are also roof hatches.

An Austrian Army APC variant, the first **Pandur** production model ordered in 1994 and intended for United Nations duties, has a raised rear hull roof to increase internal head space for the eight troops carried, plus an externally mounted and protected 12.7 mm Browning M2 MG over the commander's cupola; the initial order was for 68 units although

the final totals for this variant could be much higher.

Turreted versions of the **Pandur** are several, one being the MICV 127 carrying a one-man turret armed with one 12.7 and one 7.62 mm MG, while another model has been demonstrated carrying a two man turret armed with a Mauser 30 mm cannon.

A fire support version has been armed with various types of 90 mm gun intended for the support of armoured reconnaissance units. The all-steel welded hull configuration (two hull lengths are available) allows the **Pandur**

to be configured for many roles, typical weapon fits being an 81 mm mortar firing through hull roof hatches, an anti-tank guided missile turret, or an air defence gun or missile turret.

An ARV model is under development as is a command vehicle, along with carriers for various electronic warfare (EW) suites or similar specialised systems. Firm orders for these latter variants have yet to be placed although they are anticipated.

Licence production in Greece is planned.

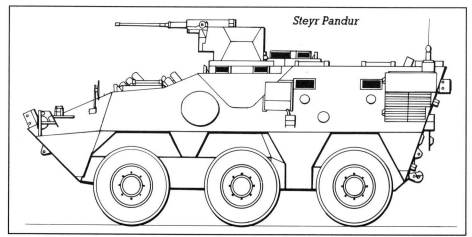

Steyr Pandur

Specification

Crew: 2
Seating: 8
Weight: (combat) 13,000 kg
Length: 5.7 m
Width: 2.5 m
Height: (hull) 1.82 m
Ground clearance: 0.43 m
Track: 2.148 m
Max speed: (road) 100 km/h
Fuel capacity: 295 litres
Range: 600 km
Fording: 1.2 m
Vertical obstacle: 0.5 m
Engine: Steyr WD diesel
Power output: 260 hp
Suspension: independent
Armament: see text
Variants: APC, MICV 127, fire support vehicle, mortar carrier, missile carrier, ambulance, command, etc.

The Steyr Pandur configured as a reconnaissance vehicle armed with a 90 mm gun.

Saurer 4K 4FA APC   Austria

The first prototype of the **Saurer 4K 4FA** series was produced in 1958, to be followed by a series of 'product improved' prototypes which differed mainly in having increasingly powerful engines until the 250 hp **4K 4FA** series emerged.

The series remained in production until 1969 by which time Saurer had been taken over by Steyr-Daimler-Puch and a series of variants with designations of bewildering complexity had appeared; the final production total was 445, all of them going to the Austrian Army.

The base vehicle is a turretless APC based on a well-sloped welded steel hull with the front plates proof against 20 mm projectiles and with internal provision for eight soldiers plus the two-man crew (commander and driver); the main armament is a 12.7 mm Browning M2 MG over the commander's cupola while 7.62 mm MGs can be mounted on various roof locations close to the troop compartment roof hatches.

A close variant has a small turret armed with a 20 mm Oerlikon cannon which can be used against ground and air targets. An 81 mm mortar carrier, converted from APCs, fires through open roof hatches and there is also a rocket launcher variant launching Oerlikon magazine-fed 81 mm rockets from two barrels mounted on a turntable.

At least four special-purpose models exist, fitted out for high level commanders, air defence or artillery commanders, or various communications equipments. There is also an unarmed ambulance model.

Several experimental models, such as a 120 mm mortar carrier and a flamethrower model, were not proceeded with.

All the **4K 4FA** variants tend to demonstrate their age by their lack of NBC protection systems for the occupants and crew, no provision for night vision equipment (other than hand-held units) and by not being amphibious. However, despite having been superseded by the Steyr 4K 7FA series (see following entry) there are plans to upgrade the **4K 4FA** units to enable them to remain operational until the late 1990s at least.

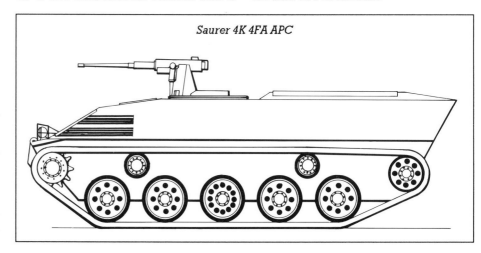

Saurer 4K 4FA APC

Specification

Crew: 2
Seating: 8
Weight: (combat, 20 mm turret) 15,000 kg
Length: 5.4 m
Width: 2.5 m
Height: (hull) 1.65 m
Ground clearance: 0.42 m
Track: 2.12 m
Max speed: (road) 65 km/h
Fuel capacity: 184 litres
Range: 370 km
Fording: 1 m

Vertical obstacle: 0.8 m
Engine: Sauer Model 4FA diesel
Power output: 250 hp
Suspension: torsion bar
Armament: 1 x 12.7 mm MG or 20 mm cannon
Variants: see text

Side view of the Saurer 4K 4FA APC.

Steyr 4K 7FA APC   Austria, Greece

The **Steyr 4K 7FA** series may be regarded as an updated version of the Saurer 4K 4FA (see previous entry) and is provided with extra armour, a more powerful engine and other changes.

The overall layout and appearance of the **4K 7FA** are very similar to the earlier model but detail changes include the provision of a collective NBC system, improved internal ventilation and an automatic fire prevention system.

The first example, the 4K 7FA G127, appeared in 1976, with production commencing the following year. This is the base APC model carrying two crew and eight troops. It is armed with a 12.7 mm Browning MG over the commander's cupola and there are ball-type firing ports in the walls of the troop compartment to allow the occupants to utilise their personal weapons. There is also an arrangement which allows 7.62 mm MGs to be fired from around the open roof hatches. Variants follow the same general lines as the **4K 4FA** series and include an 81 mm mortar carrier, a command version with extra radios and other command equipment, and an unarmed armoured ambulance for two stretcher cases plus four seated casualties.

Various other models have been produced in one-off form, including one with a 30 mm cannon one-man turret, various 20 and 30 mm air defence gun systems, and a fire support vehicle with a 90 mm gun turret.

Unlike the previous model, the **4K 7FA** has achieved a degree of export success with sales to Bolivia (6) and Nigeria (170). The vehicle is licence produced in Greece where it is known as the **Leonidas.**

About 200 units have been produced by ELBO for the Greek Army, plus a further undetermined quantity for Cyprus.

The Leonidas has been trialled carrying a number of turret designs mounting 25 mm cannon as a possible solution to a Greek Army requirement for an AIFV.

Trials have also been conducted with a **Leonidas** carrying a 90 mm gun turret.

The outcome of these trials has yet to be announced.

Production in Austria has ceased but could be restarted if further orders materialise.

Production is still under way in Greece.

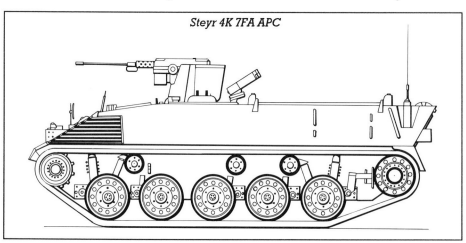

Steyr 4K 7FA APC

Specification

Crew: 2
Seating: 8
Weight: (combat) 14,800 kg
Length: 5.87 m
Width: 2.5 m
Height: 1.61 m
Ground clearance: 0.42 m
Track: 2.12 m
Max speed: (road) 70 km/h
Fuel capacity: 360 litres
Range: 520 km
Fording: 1 m
Vertical obstacle: 0.8 m
Engine: Steyr 7FA turbo diesel
Power output: 320 hp
Suspension: torsion bar
Armament: 12.7 mm MG or 20 mm cannon
Variants: See text, Leonidas APC

The Leonidas, the license-produced version of the Steyr 4K 7FA APC.

BDX APC   Belgium

The **BDX APC** is the result of a licence agreement between Beherman Demoen of Belgium and an Irish holding company to manufacture the Timoney 4 x 4 wheeled APC in Belgium. The result, the **BDX**, first produced in 1977, is based on an Irish design which has been produced in Ireland in limited numbers for the Irish Army. The Belgian **BDX** has been produced for both the Belgian Air Force (43) and the State Gendarmerie (80), while a further five have been supplied to Argentina.

While the **BDX** is essentially similar to the Timoney some changes were introduced to suit Belgian requirements. The basic **BDX APC** does not have a turret, being an armoured steel hull with access doors in the sides and rear. The troop compartment can accommodate up to 10 occupants, all provided with individual seating; an NBC collective protection or air conditioning system can be added.

Some vehicles have a small dozer blade at the front for obstacle clearing. One unusual feature of the **BDX** is that, despite its bulk, it is amphibious, propulsion when in the water being supplied from the wheels although water jet units can be fitted to improve performance. A total of 13 of the Belgian Gendarmerie vehicles are fitted with an 81 mm mortar firing to the rear through roof hatches. It is also possible to instal a small turret on the forward hull roof to accommodate either one or two 7.62 mm MGs. Other turreted weapons could include 20 mm cannon, a breech-loaded 81 mm mortar, or a 90 mm gun.

Various other variants have been proposed, including turreted anti-tank missile-carriers, an ambulance and a 51 mm MRL. A diesel engine has been tested as a possible option.

Since the **BDX** entered service numerous modifications and improvements, such as a revised suspension to allow greater weights to be carried and a revised front hull to provide the driver with more space, have been incorporated into an upgraded model known as the **Valkyr.** This variant is now produced in the United Kingdom by Vickers Defence Systems.

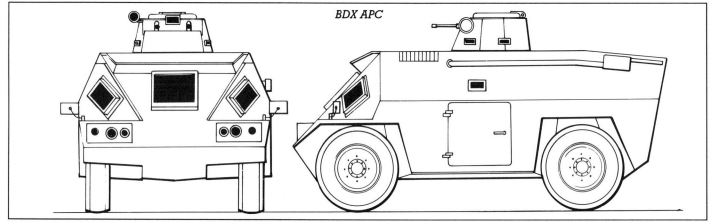

BDX APC

A Belgian manufactured version of the BDX.

Specification

Crew: 2
Seating: up to 10
Weight: (combat) 10,700 kg
Length: 5.05 m
Width: 2.5 m
Height: (hull) 2.06 m
Ground clearance: 0.4 m
Track: 1.93 m
Max speed: (road) 100 km/h
Fuel capacity: 248 litres
Range: up to 900 km
Fording: amphibious
Vertical obstacle: 0.4 m
Engine: Chrysler V-8 petrol
Power output: 180 hp
Suspension: independent
Armament: see text
Variants: Timoney, Valkyr - also see text

ENGESA EE-11 Urutu APC   Brazil

At one time it seemed very likely that the Brazilian **EE-11 Urutu** APC would become one of the most numerous of all current military vehicles.

First run out by ENGESA during 1970, the Brazilian Army placed an order and from 1974 onwards further orders came in from all around the world, one of the most significant being a large order from Iraq.

Based around components also employed in the design of the ENGESA EE-9 armoured car, including the 'boomerang' rear suspension, the **EE-11 Urutu** is a simple and unsophisticated 6 x 6 design with a spacious passenger compartment entered through a single door at the rear; troop loads can vary from 8 to 12 and roof hatches are provided.

Although relatively bulky the vehicle is amphibious. The **Urutu** was designed to be a relatively low cost APC capable of being produced in a variety of forms from the basic APC with only 7.62 or 12.7 mm MGs for armament to a fire support vehicle armed with an ENGESA 90 mm gun. Other armaments have included turreted 60 mm breech-loaded mortars and 20 or 25 mm cannon. Also produced have been 81 mm mortar carriers, command versions with extra radios, ambulance models with a raised roof to increase internal space, and a variant capable of recovering and repairing damaged or stranded vehicles.

There was also an armoured cargo carrier capable of carrying 2 tonnes of ammunition or other front line supplies in the seatless troop compartment. An internal security/riot control model with a front-mounted obstacle-clearing dozer blade was also produced, some being ordered by Jordan.

Exports to nations as disparate as Angola, Cyprus, Libya and Venezuela were made, the latter nation alone ordering 100 units.

In all some 17 nations ordered the **Urutu** in one form or another. However, with the end of the Iran-Iraq war, one of the largest customers, Iraq, was no longer in the market. ENGESA subsequently contracted financial difficulties and production of all ENGESA vehicles and other defence products ceased.

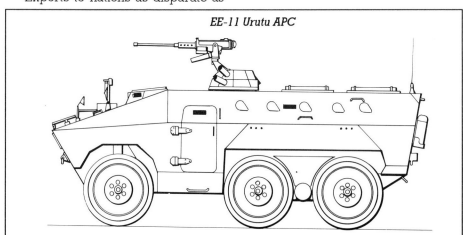

EE-11 Urutu APC

Specification

Crew: 1 or 2
Seating: up to 12
Weight: (combat) 14,000 kg
Length: 6.1 m
Width: 2.65 m
Height: (hull) 2.125 m
Ground clearance: 0.38 m
Track: 2.2 m
Max speed: (road) 105 km/h
Fuel capacity: 380 litres
Range: 850 km
Fording: amphibious
Vertical obstacle: 0.6 m
Engine: Detroit Diesel 6V-53T diesel
Power output: 260 hp
Suspension: front independent, rear, boomerang
Armament: see text
Variants: Many - see text

The Brazilian Urutu 6x6 APC seen here armed with a 12.7 mm MG.

Light Armored Vehicle (LAV) 25   Canada

The **Light Armored Vehicle**, or **LAV,** is an 8 x 8 variant of the MOWAG Piranha licence produced by General Motors of Canada for the US Marine Corps, the US Army, Australia (who obtained 15 before ordering the Bison) and Saudi Arabia.

The **LAV** closely follows the overall layout of the Swiss Piranha, as do the 6 x 6 Canadian armed forces models which are named the **Husky**. The total of 758 8 x 8 LAVs for the US Marine Corps include the **LAV-25** APC with a 25 mm cannon in a turret, the **LAV(R)** recovery vehicle, the **LAV(L)** supply carrier, the **LAV(M)** 81 mm mortar carrier, the **LAV(C)** command vehicle and the **LAV(AT)** with TOW anti-tank missiles carried on a roof-mounted twin missile launcher. Other proposed **LAV** variants for the Saudi Arabian National Guard order (which stands at a total of 1,117 of all types) include a 120 mm mortar carrier (probably with a breech-loaded mortar in a turret), an air defence version with a combined gun and missile armament, and an assault gun carrying a 90 mm gun; a 105 mm tank gun version of the latter has been proposed. From these initial models have emerged a host of others with the basic LAV's capacious hull being configured, for example, to accommodate electronic warfare (EW) suites while others are equipped as long range reconnaissance vehicles. There has even been a proposed 'disrupter' version to clear unexploded ordnance from airfields but the development funds were withdrawn. An NBC reconnaissance version has been produced but was not proceeded with. **LAVs** in service have undergone some modification and armour-increase projects involving armour tiles.

Further enhancement programmes may include increased tyre widths with tyre chains to enable them to cross soft terrain or beaches, and (possibly) an increase in engine output. **LAVs** are air-transportable and have been para-dropped. Many saw action in Grenada and during Operation Desert Storm.

For details of the visually similar **Bison**, refer to the following entry.

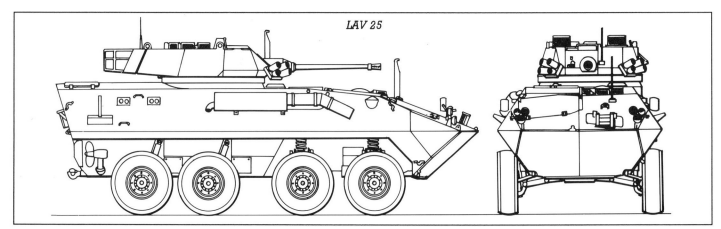

LAV 25

Specification

Crew: 3
Seating: 6
Weight: (combat) 12,792 kg
Length: 6.393 m
Width: 2.5 m
Height: 2.7 m
Ground clearance: 0.39 m
Max speed: (road) 100 km/h
Fuel capacity: 204 litres
Range: 668 km
Fording: amphibious
Vertical obstacle: 0.5 m
Engine: Detroit Diesel 6V-53T diesel
Power output: 275 hp
Suspension: independent
Armament: 1 x 25 mm cannon,
        1 x 7.62 mm MG
Variants: Many (see text), including Bison

The LAV-25 IFV, base model of the Light Armoured Vehicle (LAV) family.

The **Bison** is a Canadian-developed 8 x 8 variant of the MOWAG Piranha produced in Canada as the 8 x 8 Light Armored Vehicle (LAV -see previous entry). Developed within the very short time scale of seven days by General Motors of Canada, the first **Bison** appeared in 1988 with production commencing the following year.

The main customer to date has been the Canadian Armed Forces who ordered 199 for the Militia, with Australia ordering a further 97. About 12 have been loaned to the US National Guard to support anti-drug operations.

The **Bison** follows the same general lines as the 6 x 6 Piranha but with many detail differences, the main one being a rail system along the floor which allows entire suites of equipment to be removed or installed within a short time to permit the base vehicle to be used for many roles.

As an APC the **Bison** can carry eight troops but the seating arrangements can slide out through the large power-operated ramp at the rear and be replaced with one of several alternatives. These include a command post with extra radios and other command equipment, and an 81 mm mortar platform with ammunition racking. One variant without the quick-change installations forms what is termed a Mobile Repair Team. This variant has a two-man crew provided with various vehicle repair tools, spare and other equipment while on the roof is a hydraulic crane for the recovery of light vehicles or to lift engine packs.

Australian **Bison** variants include ambulances and what are termed surveillance vehicles, the latter being used to patrol large areas of outback or coastline. Although the armament of most Canadian **Bisons** is limited to a 7.62 mm MG over the commander's hatch, plus the occupants' weapons, some Australian **Bisons** have a 25 mm cannon in a small turret. The **Bison** can be rendered fully amphibious after about two minutes preparation.

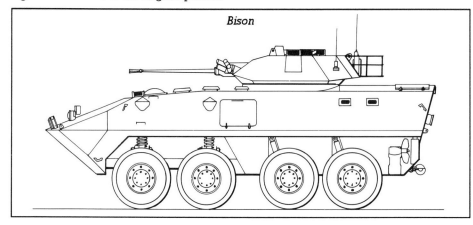

Bison

Specifications:

Crew: 2
Seating: 8
Weight: (combat) 12,395 kg
Length: 6.452 m
Width: 2.5 m
Height: 2.21 m
Ground clearance: 0.39 m
Track: not known
Max speed: (road) 100 km/h
Fuel capacity: variable
Range: 665 km
Fording: amphibious
Vertical obstacle: up to 0.5 m
Engine: Detroit Diesel 6V53T diesel
Power output: 275 hp
Suspension: independent
Armament: 7.62 mm MG
Variants: See text

The base model APC version of the Canadian Bison.

The Soviet **BMP-1** IFV (qv) became one of the most influential of Soviet post-war armoured vehicle designs, having been either directly copied or licence-produced by several countries, a typical example of the latter being the Romanian **MLI-84**. The Chinese also decided to produce the type but their starting point was reportedly a **BMP-1** supplied to China via Egypt. Once acquired, the original was dismantled and copied, with various local modifications being introduced to meet local requirements and manufacturing methods. The end result, the Type **WZ 501** IFV, thus visually resembles the **BMP-1** but there are numerous detail differences between the two.

The base Type **WZ 501** retains the same 73 mm low velocity gun and locally-produced 9K11 Malyutka-derived anti-tank missile armament as the Soviet original, along with the same cramped internal layout while the later Type **WZ 501A** has a more effective 25 mm cannon and a co-axial 7.62 mm MG in a turret identical to that employed on the Type WZ 551 APC (qv). The revised Type WZ 503 changed things around with seats along the hull walls (in the Type **WZ 501** the troops are seated centrally, back-to-back, to face outwards); the armament is limited to an externally mounted 12.7 mm MG. The Type WZ 504 has a turret-like housing mounting four Red

Arrow anti-tank missiles.

The Type WZ 505 is an armoured ambulance with a two-man crew, air conditioning, a raised superstructure roof and internal accommodation for four stretchers.

The Type WZ 506 is a Type **WZ 501** configured as a command post vehicle. One further derivative, the NFV-1, used a Type **WZ 501** chassis allied to an American-designed turret armed with a 25 mm cannon - it did not pass the prototype stage. Despite some marketing attempts the Type **WZ 501** series was not sold outside China and is used only by the Chinese armed forces.

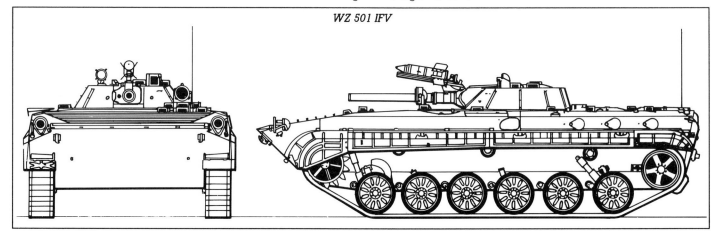

WZ 501 IFV

Specification

Crew: 3
Seating: 8
Weight: (combat) 13,300 kg
Length: 6.74 m
Width: 2.97 m
Height: 2.158 m
Ground clearance: 0.38 m
Track: approx 2.7 m
Max speed: (road) 65 km/h
Fuel capacity: approx 450 litres
Range: approx 500 km
Fording: amphibious
Vertical obstacle: up to 0.8 m
Engine: Type 6V-150 diesel
Power output: 298 hp
Suspension: torsion bar
Armament: 1 x 73 mm gun, 1 x 7.62 mm MG, 1 x ATGW launcher
Variants: Types WZ 501A, 503, 504, 505, 506

Rear view of a Type WZ 503 IFV, one of the vehicles in the Chinese type WZ 501 IFV family.

The **Type 77** tracked APC was manufactured by China North Industries, universally known as NORINCO. It originated as a copy of the Soviet BTR-50P APC but the **Type 77** version displays numerous differences and is powered by a more powerful diesel engine which imparts a better all-round performance; many of the **Type 77**'s components are also used for the Type 63 light tank.

The layout of the **Type 77** is simple and basic, with the crew compartment forward, the main troop-carrying compartment in the centre and the engine compartment at the rear; the 16 troops carried enter and leave via roof hatches. Armament is limited to a single unprotected 12.7 mm MG located over the commander's roof hatch but there are firing ports for some of the occupants along the hull sides.

The **Type 77** is fully amphibious following minimal preparation, propulsion once in the water being provided by twin water jets located at the rear.

As well as being configured as an APC the empty **Type 77** may be employed as a forward area load carrier or fuel supply vehicle. With a special artillery variant known as the **Type 77-1** the roof may be used to carry a 122 mm field howitzer or an 85mm anti-tank gun, their crews and a quantity of ammunition. The pieces are loaded onto the roof from the rear via three ramps which can be carried slung along the hull sides when not in use.

A **Type 77-2** carries artillery ammunition and may act as an artillery tractor.

The base **Type 77** is also employed in a modified non-amphibious form to carry the HQ-2J surface-to-air missile, a copy of the old Soviet SA-2.

Other **Type 77** variants include an armoured ambulance and the usual command and control version provided with extra radios.

Production of the **Type 77** ceased some years ago and the series remains in service only with the Chinese Army.

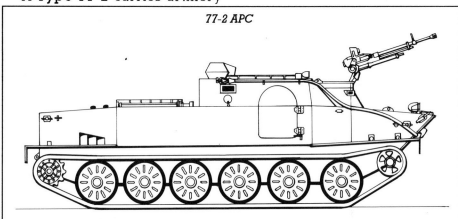

77-2 APC

Specification

Crew: 2
Seating: 16
Weight: (combat) approx 15,500 kg
Length: 7.4 m
Width: 3.2 m
Height: 2.436 m
Ground clearance: approx 0.3 m
Track: 2.8 m
Max speed: (road) 60 km/h
Fuel capacity: 416 litres
Range: 370 km

Fording: amphibious
Vertical obstacle: 0.87 m
Engine: Type 12150L-2A diesel
Power output: 400 hp
Suspension: torsion bar
Armament: 1 x 12.7 mm MG
Variants: Type 77-1 and 77-2; see text

The Type 77 APC, the Chinese version of the former Soviet Union BTR-50PK.

Type YW 531 APC   People's Republic of China

Development of the **Type YW 531** APC commenced during the late 1960s and was an entirely Chinese project involving German Deutz diesel power packs. This vehicle has been known by other designations such as K-63 or Type 63 and at one time was known in the West as the M1967 from the first year in which it was observed. The overall design is basic, being little more than an armoured steel box on tracks. There are only four road wheels each side but the cross country performance is stated to be excellent and the overall design is robust and adaptable, even if some refinements such as an NBC protection system are absent.

Apart from large scale service with the Chinese armed forces the **Type YW 531** has seen action with the North Vietnamese Army, with Zaire forces in Angola, and with the Tanzanian Army against Uganda. A batch was also delivered to Iraq at one point.

Other nations known to be using the **Type YW 531** include Albania, the Sudan and North Korea. As an APC the **YW 531** series is armed with a single external 12.7 mm MG, although only one sub-version provides any protection for the gunner. Various sub-variants with differing communication suites have been observed (Types YW 531C, D and E, all APCs). The Type YW 701 is a command post vehicle while the Type YW 304 is an 82 mm mortar carrier; the Type YW 381 carries a 120 mm mortar. A much revised and longer variant known as the Type 54-1 self-propelled howitzer carries a 122 mm artillery piece while another artillery variant, the Type 70 MRL, carries a 19-barrel rocket launcher array. The basic APC may be fitted with a small turret carrying four Red Arrow anti-tank missiles ready to launch plus further reload missiles inside the hull.

Other variants, such as a propaganda vehicle with loudspeakers, are known to exist. Production of the Type **YW 531** has now ceased in favour of the Type YW 534 (next entry).

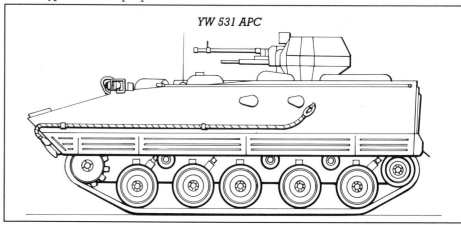
YW 531 APC

Specification:

(Type YW 531C)

Crew: 2
Seating: 13
Weight: (combat) 12,600 kg
Length: 5.475 m
Width: 2.978 m
Height: (hull top) 1.887 m
Ground clearance: 0.45 m
Track: 2.464 m
Max speed: (road) 65 km/h
Fuel capacity: 450 litres
Range: 500 km
Fording: amphibious
Vertical obstacle: 0.6 m
Engine: Deutz BF8L413F diesel
Power output: 320 hp
Suspension: torsion bar
Armament: 1 x 12.7 mm MG
Variants: See text

Type YW 531 APCs during the final phases of an infantry attack.

YW 534 APC

The tracked Type **YW 534** APC is understood to be the successor to the Type YW 531 series (see previous entry) and the type has many design details in common with the very similar Type 531 H APC (also known as the Type 85), some of which have been sold to Thailand, but the **Type YW 534** is slightly larger overall. Both are manufactured by NORINCO but are powered by German Deutz diesels.

The base model of the **Type YW 534** is fully amphibious with propulsion once in the water being provided by the tracks. Troops enter the vehicle via a single door in the hull rear. Once inside there are several ball-and-socket firing ports for the occupants, one being in the entry door, and periscopes are provided to allow observation of the outside world by the crew compartment occupants.

A collective NBC protection system is provided for both the crew and occupants. The main armament on the **Type YW 534** APC remains a single 12.7 mm MG located over a forward roof hatch for air and local defence.

On the Type YW 307 IFV, a variant of the **Type YW 534**, the main armament is increased to an externally mounted 25 mm cannon with a coaxial 7.62 mm MG. Inside the Type YW 307 IFV the number of troops carried is reduced to seven (plus the driver and commander) although the combat weight is increased to 15,400 kg. There is also a Red Arrow anti-tank guided missile carrier variant of the **Type YW 534** which carries over the same four-missile turret launching arrangements as the earlier Type 531 (qv); extra missiles are carried inside the hull for reloading once the turret has been lowered into the raised roof superstructure over the rear hull.

As far as is known the **Type YW 534** is in service only with the Chinese Army.

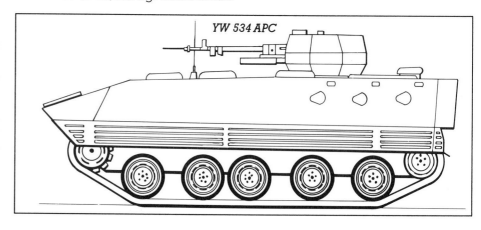

YW 534 APC

The external 25 mm cannon marks this IFV as the YW 307, the IFV model of the Type YW 534 family.

Specification

Crew: 2
Seating: 13
Weight: (combat) 14,300 kg
Length: 6.15 m
Width: 3.134 m
Height: (hull top) 1.88 m
Ground clearance: 0.48 m
Track: 2.626 m
Max speed: (road) 65 km/h
Fuel capacity: not known
Range: 500 km
Fording: amphibious
Vertical obstacle: 0.7 m
Engine: Deutz BF8L413F diesel
Power output: 320 hp
Suspension: torsion bar
Armament: 1 x 12.7 mm MG
Variants: YW 307 IFV, see also text

Type WZ 551 APC and IFV   People's Republic of China

The **Type WZ 551** series of wheeled APCs and IFVs was first shown in prototype form by NORINCO in 1986. At that time many observed that the overall design resembled that of the French Renault VAB (qv) but subsequent investigations have shown that although there may have been some French influence the **Type WZ 551** has many differences in overall dimensions, weights and many other aspects.

To date only 6 x 6 configurations of the **Type WZ 551** have been observed although it has been stated that 4 x 4 and 8 x 8 versions are under development. The overall layout and form of the Type WZ 551 follows that of the VAB, with one variant, the NGV-1 IFV, being fitted with a French Giat Industries one-man turret mounting a 25 mm cannon. The more usual IFV armament is a 25 mm cannon on an external turret mounting, the same mounting being also used on the Type YW 307 IFV (see previous entry) and the Type WZ 501A (qv). Other weapon installations have included

the 73 mm low velocity gun turret from the Type WZ 501 IFV base model (qv). The base model **Type WZ 551** APC, which is amphibious, is armed with a single 12.7 mm MG and can carry up to 11 fully equipped troops.

One variant, which may already have seen combat, has been reported to be in service with the Bosnian Army in small numbers. This is an anti-tank vehicle carrying four Red Arrow missiles on a small launcher turret; ground mountings are carried for off-vehicle

launching. One further variant on a lengthened 6 x 6 chassis is understood to mount a self-propelled 122 mm howitzer; this extended chassis has also been proposed as a mobile air defence gun mounting.

The **Type WZ 551** APC and 25 mm cannon IFV are understood to be in service with the Chinese armed forces and will doubtless be joined by other models as they emerge.

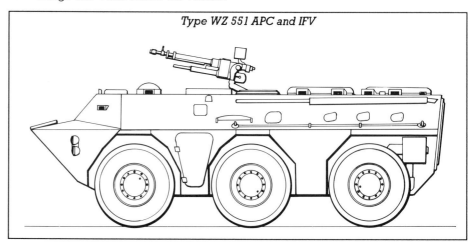

Type WZ 551 APC and IFV

Specification

(25 mm IFV)
Crew: 3 (2 on APC)
Seating: 9 (11 on APC)
Weight: (combat) 15,300 kg
Length: 6.65 m
Width: 2.8 m
Height: (hull top) 1.95 m
Ground clearance: 0.41 m
Track: 2.44 m
Max speed: (road) 85 km/h
Fuel capacity: not known
Range: approx 600 km
Fording: amphibious
Vertical obstacle: 0.5 m
Engine: Deutz BF8L413F diesel
Power output: 256 hp
Suspension: coil springs
Armament: 1 x 25 mm cannon;
1 x 7.62 mm MG
Variants: See text

Side view of the NORINCO Type WZ 551 wheeled APC.

WZ 523 APC

When the **Type WZ 523** wheeled APC was first displayed in public in late 1984 there were many observations regarding its design origins for it closely resembles the South African Ratel (qv).

As with the Type WZ 551 APC/IFV (previous entry), these similarities are misleading for there are many differences from the Ratel on the 6 x 6 **Type WZ 523**, one being the driving position. On the Ratel this is a one-man central position while on the **Type WZ 523** the driver sits next to the commander.

The location of the main roof-located weapon station also differs and on the **Type WZ 523** is further back, limited (on the base model at least) to a single 12.7 mm MG.

There are many other detail differences, especially in the lower hull shapes, so the **Type WZ 523** can probably lay claim to being a home-based Chinese design with only slight influence from elsewhere.

When it was first observed this vehicle was given the Western designation of M1984 APC and many American references still use this title.

The **Type WZ 523** is a Second Automobile Plant product (although it is marketed by NORINCO) which to date has only been observed in APC form, carrying up to ten fully equipped troops who enter their compartment via a single door in the hull rear; roof hatches are provided.

The vehicle is fully amphibious after a trim vane has been raised on the hull front. Once in the water propulsion at speeds up to 7 km/h is provided by two water jets in the hull rear. The basic APC could be readily converted for the command vehicle or armoured ambulance roles, as well as to turretless mortar or anti-tank missile carriers.

As far as is known the **Type WZ 523** APC is in service only with the Chinese Army and is understood to be still in production.

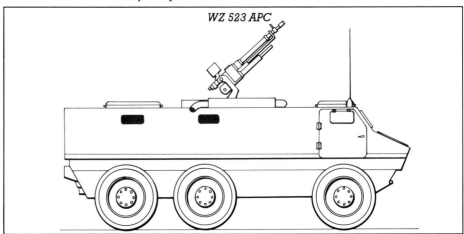

WZ 523 APC

Specification

Crew: 2
Seating: 10
Weight: (combat) 11,200 kg
Length: 6.02 m
Width: 2.55 m
Height: (overall) 2.73 m
Ground clearance: approx 0.3 m
Track: not known
Max speed: (road) 80 km/h
Fuel capacity: 255 litres
Range: 600 km
Fording: amphibious
Vertical obstacle: approx 0.5 m
Engine: EQ 6105 petrol
Power output: 165 hp
Suspension: independent
Armament: 1 x 12.7 mm MG
Variants: None known - see text

One of the few shots available of the Type WZ 523 wheeled APV, seen here on parade in Beijing.

BMP-1 IFV

The **BMP-1** was first shown publicly in 1967 and created quite a stir in the West by its apparent combination of mobility and gun/missile firepower. Time was to demonstrate that, despite its many innovations, the **BMP-1** was not the wonder vehicle it first appeared to be for its low silhouette had to be paid for by a cramped interior for the occupants and the main armament was not as powerful as was at first thought. The armament emerged as a magazine fed low velocity 73 mm gun with poor accuracy at longer ranges and a barrel-mounted 9K11 wire-guided missile with an indifferent performance - on many later models the missile was completely removed.

But in its day the BMP-1 was the vehicle that others were measured by and the type was churned out in thousands in the former Soviet Union and Czechoslovakia.

From those two nations sprang a whole host of variants to meet just about every combat requirement from artillery observation to armoured engineering vehicle (AEV).

Many vehicles were fitted with extra armour or had more powerful engines installed, while the Chinese produced their WZ 501 copy (qv). **BMP-1**s were exported to many nations and remain in service in large numbers, having seen combat in Afghanistan, the Middle East (including the Iran-Iraq War),

Chad and Angola.

In all these areas the **BMP-1** proved to be a rugged, serviceable vehicle but the limited internal dimensions were always a drawback, despite the provision of two rear entry doors, roof hatches, firing ports and other measures which made the **BMP-1** a true infantry fighting vehicle.

There have been many detail changes during the **BMP-1**'s production life and, despite production having ceased, new variants continue to appear, one of the latest being a Czech NBC reconnaissance vehicle; many of these variants are purely local modifications to meet some local need.

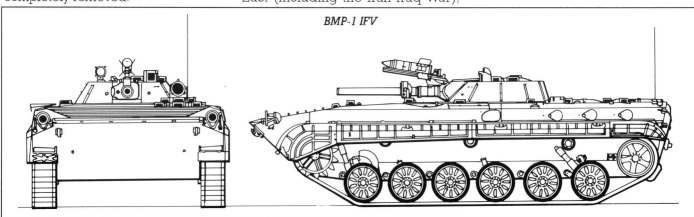

BMP-1 IFV

Specification

Crew: 3
Seating: 8
Weight: (combat) approx 13,500 kg
Length: 6.74 m
Width: 2.94 m
Height: (overall) 2.15 m
Ground clearance: 0.39 m
Track: 2.75 m
Max speed: (road) 65 km/h
Fuel capacity: 460 litres
Range: approx 600 km
Fording: amphibious

Vertical obstacle: 0.8 m
Engine: Type UTD-20 diesel
Power output: 300 hp
Suspension: torsion bar
Armament: 1 x 73 mm gun; 1 x 7.62 mm MG; 9K11 ATGW
Variants: Many - see text

The IFV which startled the West: the BMP-1 armed with a 73 mm gun, an ATGW and the crew's personal weapons.

BMP-2 IFV   Former Soviet Union

The **BMP-2** IFV first appeared in the late 1970s and may be regarded as a 'product improved' BMP-1 (previous entry). Many of the drawbacks of the BMP-1 were eliminated, the most obvious being the replacement of the BMP-1's 73 mm low velocity gun by a more versatile and effective 30 mm cannon and the relocation of the commander from a position behind the driver to the turret.

ATGW launchers may be mounted over the turret and an anti-tank grenade launcher is often carried. The rather cramped interior remains but the number of troops carried is reduced to seven (plus the commander who normally dismounts with the troops). The **BMP-2** has been produced in large numbers; the Russian Army alone is estimated to have received some 20,000 vehicles so the type remains one of the Eastern Bloc's most important combat vehicles numerically. Licence production continues in the former Czechoslovakia (BVP-2) and in India, where the **BMP-2** is known as the Sarath. Essentially similar vehicles have been produced in Bulgaria (BMP-30) from where many were exported to Iraq.

The **BMP-2** carries over the same general lines as the BMP-1 and is thus a low, agile, reliable and serviceable vehicle with adequate engine power for most all-terrain missions, especially with late production vehicles which have several improvements over earlier models such as improved fire control, extra armour in places and layout alterations.

A command version exists and mine ploughs may be fitted to most vehicles. Indian Sarath variants include an armoured ambulance, an armoured engineering vehicle and a bridging reconnaissance vehicle.

The **BMP-2** is still in production and is still offered for export sales. It is already in service with Finland, Iraq, the Yemen, Poland, Kuwait, Jordan, Afghanistan and Algeria, as well as India, the Czech Republic and Slovakia.

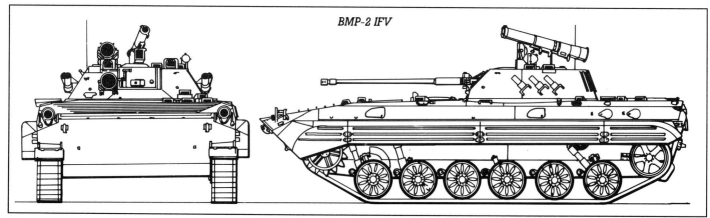

BMP-2 IFV

Specification

Crew: 3
Seating: 7
Weight: (combat) 14,300 kg
Length: 6.735 m
Width: 3.15 m
Height: 2.45 m
Ground clearance: 0.42 m
Track: 2.55 m
Max speed: (road) 65 km/h
Fuel capacity: 462 litres
Range: approx. 600 km
Fording: amphibious
Vertical obstacle: 0.7 m
Engine: Model UTD-20 diesel
Power output: 300 hp
Suspension: torsion bar
Armament: 1 x 30 mm cannon;
1 x 7.62 mm MG; ATGW
Variants: Sarath -also see text

The main visual feature which differentiates the BMP-2 IFV (seen here) from the BMP-1 is the 30 mm main armament.

The **BMP-3** IFV entered service with the Russian Army in 1990 and immediately created a stir in Western armoured circles as it was obvious that the design owed nothing to previous models; for a while the type was given the Western designation of M1990/1.

Overall, the **BMP-3** resembles a lightly-armoured light tank and is bulky and rather high but its main attribute seems to be a 100 mm gun capable of firing automatically-loaded laser-guided anti-armour projectiles as well as FRAG-HE; the 100 mm 9M117 'Bastion' laser-guided projectile has a potential combat range of 4,000 metres, allowing the **BMP-3** to have a considerable anti-armour potential. There is also a coaxial 30 mm cannon and 7.62 mm MG plus two fixed bow-mounted 7.62 mm MGs firing forward.

The troops carried are located around the vehicle, one each side of the driver with the rest seated to the rear in two rows over the engine pack on two inward-facing bench seats with limited head room. Despite its weight (18.7 tonnes) the **BMP-3** is fully amphibious with water propulsion provided by two water jet units in the hull rear. A reconnaissance version with the 100 mm gun removed (but retaining the 30 mm cannon) has been observed in prototype form and it has been proposed that the turretless **BMP-3** chassis could be utilised as the basis for a series of variants such as an ARV - a driver training version has also been mooted along with an air defence version mounting a French missile turret.

Despite its many innovations the **BMP-3** has yet to enter service in large numbers with the Russian Army, probably due to the high costs involved, but export orders have been placed by Abu Dhabi and Kuwait, some of the latter order, which may reach 500 units, being fitted with French fire control systems.

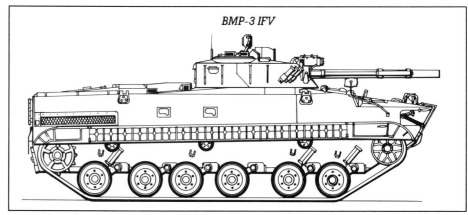

BMP-3 IFV

Specification:

Crew: 3
Seating: 7
Weight: (combat) 18,700 kg
Length: 7.2 m
Width: 3.23 m
Height: (overall) 3.23 m
Ground clearance: 0.45 m
Track: 2.76 m
Max speed: (road) 70 km/h
Fuel capacity: not known
Range: approx. 600 km
Fording: amphibious
Vertical obstacle: 0.8 m
Engine: Type UTD-29M diesel
Power output: 500 hp
Suspension: torsion bar
Armament: 1 x 100 mm gun; 1 x 30 mm cannon; 3 x 7.62 mm MG
Variants: Reconnaissance version

The bulk of the BMP-3 IFV can be appreciated in this view - note the hull-mounted MG.

BMD-1 ACV

Compared to the other Eastern Bloc IFV/APCs the **BMD-1** ACV has been produced in relatively small numbers for the former Soviet Army Air Assault Divisions.

First seen in 1973, the **BMD-1** is a very lightly armoured vehicle with only a limited combat capacity but capable of supporting airborne troops during the early phases of airborne operations. For this role the main emphasis is on direct fire support so the **BMD-1** is fitted with the same gun as that used on the BMP-1 IFV (qv) in an essentially similar turret; the 9K11 ATGW launching rail is also provided but has been removed from later models. One feature of the **BMD-1** is its variable height

hydro-pneumatic suspension system, most likely for allowing the vehicle to be para-dropped on platforms. The road wheels are also small while the tracks are only 230 mm wide. The hull is bulky to render the vehicle amphibious but the hull space behind the turret is sufficient for only three personnel. Two more are seated each side of the driver while the turret houses only the gunner.

The 73 mm gun has a coaxial 7.62 mm MG while two more 7.62 mm MGs are fixed for firing from the front hull; a 30 mm grenade launcher on a ground mounting is also carried as standard.

On the BDM-2 the 73 mm gun is replaced by a 30 mm cannon; from 1990

onwards a new BDM-3 has appeared but is a new design overall. A lengthened turretless APC version of the BDM-1 (an extra road wheel is added each side) is known as the BTR-D - it can carry 13 troops plus the driver.

On the SO-120, also based on the **BDM-1** chassis, the turret is replaced by a breech-loaded 120 mm mortar, with no provision to carry extra troops.

Other **BDM-1** variants include various artillery observation vehicles, an ARV and a mortar carrier. BDM-1s have been exported to Iraq and India (the latter is not confirmed).

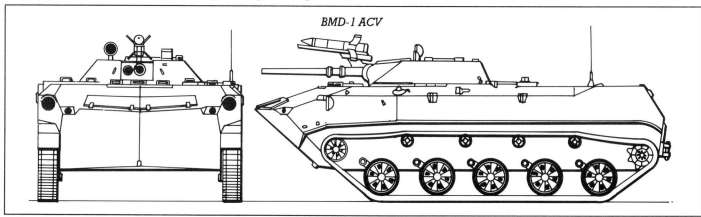

BMD-1 ACV

Specification

Crew: 3
Seating: 4
Weight: (combat) approx 7,500 kg
Length: 5.4 m
Width: 2.63 m
Height: 1.67 to 1.97 m
Ground clearance: 0.1 to 0.45 m
Track: not known
Max speed: (road) 70 km/h
Fuel capacity: 300 litres
Range: 320 km
Fording: amphibious
Vertical obstacle: approx 0.8 m
Engine: Model 5D-20 V-6 diesel
Power output: 240 hp
Suspension: hydraulic independent
Armament: 1 x 73 mm gun; 3 x 7.62 mm MG
Variants: BMD-2, BTR-D, SO-120

The diminutive BMD-1 airborne combat vehicle (ACV).

BTR-50PK
Former Soviet Union

The design of the **BTR-50P** can be traced back to the early 1950s. It has been in service so long that it is now used more as a general or special purpose carrier for systems and other applications than as an APC, although many nations continue to appreciate the vehicle's considerable troop-carrying capacity of 20 fully-equipped troops.

The **BTR-50P** is based on the chassis of the PT-76 amphibious light tank and, as an APC, seats the passengers along benches in an area behind the fully protected crew compartment, with the only armament carried being a pintle-mounted 7.62 mm MG. '

The troop compartment is open with troops having to enter and leave over the sides - the only protection against the elements is a canvas cover. On the **BTR-50PK** the troop compartment is fully enclosed, the troops entering and leaving through roof hatches. At one time ramps were provided to allow light artillery pieces to be loaded onto, and fired from, the rear hull decking but later models (BTR-50PA) lack this facility.

BTR-50P variants have been many, including command, mine-clearing, repair and recovery vehicles of various types.

A command vehicle is known as the BTR-50PU. The Chinese also produced a copy known as the Type 77 (qv) while the former Czechoslovakia produced a modified version known as the OT-62.

The **BTR-50P** series was widely exported and remains in service with many nations, so many in fact that an Israeli concern saw fit to market an updating package which included a new diesel power pack - Israel has been one of the many nations utilising the **BTR-50P.**

With many user nations the **BTR-50P** and its variants are no longer employed as front line APCs but are instead retained as front line supply and fuel carriers or have been converted to technical support vehicles to keep other vehicle types running.

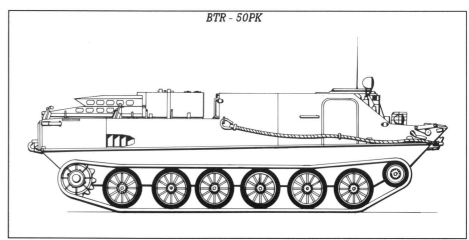

BTR - 50PK

Specification

Crew: 2
Seating: 20
Weight: (combat) 14,200 kg
Length: 7.08 m
Width: 3.14 m
Height: (hull top) 1.97 m
Ground clearance: 0.37 m
Track: 2.74 m
Max speed: (road) 44 km/h
Fuel capacity: 400 litres
Range: 400 km
Fording: amphibious
Vertical obstacle: 1.1 m
Engine: Model V-6 diesel
Power output: 240 hp
Suspension: torsion bar
Armament: 1 x 7.62 mm MG
Variants: BTR-50P, BTR-50PK, BTR-50PA, BTR-50PU, OT-62, Type 77

A Finnish army BTR-50 PK APC.

BTR-60 PB

Unlike the BTR-50P series (previous entry), the **BTR-60P** series has an 8 x 8 wheeled drive configuration, with the power being derived from two GAZ-49B petrol engines.

Entering service during the early 1960s, the original **BTR-60P** had an open troop compartment while the later (and far more numerous) **BTR-60PA** (also known as the **BTR-60PK**) had an armoured roof.

On the **BTR-60PB** a turret, mounting a 14.5 mm heavy MG and a coaxial 7.62 mm MG, was added, reducing the number of troops carried from 16 to 14.

In its day the **BTR-60** series were widely used as APCs but are now little encountered in this role. Instead the **BTR-60P** series has become a veritable maid of all work throughout the Eastern Bloc and elsewhere. Variants abound. Just to list them would fill many pages but essentially they include numerous command vehicle types, some having specialised installations for artillery or signals units, while others are equipped for various communication purposes or for electronic warfare (EW) with prominent antennae arrays. There are also artillery observation vehicles, others are front line mobile workshops, while in several Third-World nations **BTR-60P** series vehicles are employed for police or para-military duties. At least one type of forward air control post for directing strike aircraft was developed.

There have been many user nations over the years and the type can still be encountered in countries such as Cambodia, Cuba, Angola and Turkey (who received a batch of 300 ex-East German vehicles during the early 1990s); the only Warsaw Pact nations not to use the **BTR-60P** were the Czechs and the Poles. Some nations, such as Cuba, have added roof-mounted light air defence guns or recoilless anti-armour weapons.

At least 34 user nations have been identified and there may well be more.

A licence was issued to Romania to produce a **BTR-60PB**-based model known as the TAB-71, from which a 4 x 4 scout car (the TABC-79) was developed.

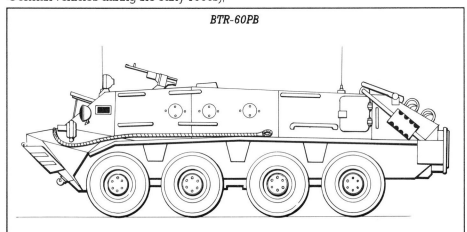

BTR-60PB

Specification
(BTR-60PB)

Crew: 2
Seating: 14
Weight: (combat) 10,300 kg
Length: 7.56 m
Width: 2.825 m
Height: (hull top) 2.055 m
Ground clearance: 0.475 m
Track: 2.37 m
Max speed: (road) 80 km/h
Fuel capacity: 290 litres
Range: 500 km

Fording: amphibious
Vertical obstacle: 0.4 m
Engine: 2 x GAZ-49B petrol
Power output: 2 x 90 hp
Suspension: torsion bar
Armament: 1 x 14.5 mm MG;
1 x 7.62 mm MG
Variants: Many - see text

BTR-60PB APCs on parade in India.

BTR-70 APC

First displayed publicly in 1978, the **BTR-70** APC may be regarded as an undated and improved version of the BTR-60P series (previous entry). For a while it was known in the West as the M1978 APC. A revised internal layout resulted in a reduction in the number of troops carried to nine while the two petrol engines were of a new and more powerful model. If either engine is damaged for any reason the vehicle can still proceed under the power of the other, although performance will be reduced. Extra armour was added, especially to the front of the hull to better protect the front wheels.

The turret and MG armament from the BTR-60PB were carried over complete, without modification, although some late production examples may be encountered with the revised turret of the BTR-80 series (see following entry). Numerous detail changes were introduced, including a better NBC protection system than that introduced to the BTR-60P series. Compared to the earlier BTR-60P series there have (as yet) been relatively few **BTR-70** variants. These have included the inevitable command vehicles (in more than one form), the **BTR-70Kh NBC** reconnaissance vehicle fitted with numerous NBC warfare agent sensors

and warning systems, and the BREM. The latter is a turretless vehicle with a small crane over the front hull for the repair of stranded vehicles in the front line.

There is also a **BTR-70MS** with the interior revised to carry various suites of communication equipment; a radar jamming vehicle is known to exist.

In Afghanistan some **BTR-70**s carried a 30 mm automatic grenade launcher on the roof behind the main turret. A licence-produced version has been produced in Romania where it is known as the TAB-77. Several variants of this model have been developed, including an artillery command post and observation vehicle.

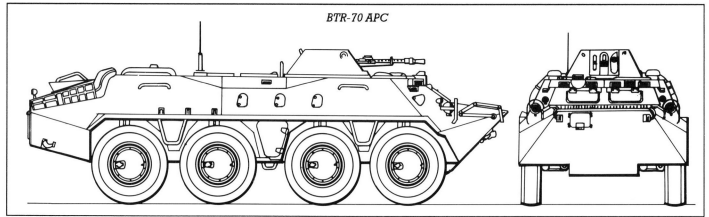

BTR-70 APC

Specification

Crew: 2
Seating: 9
Weight: (combat) approx 11,500 kg
Length: 7.535 m
Width: 2.8 m
Height: 2.235 m
Ground clearance: 0.475 m
Track: 2.38 m
Max speed: (road) 80 km/h

Fuel capacity: approx 350 litres
Range: up to 600 km
Fording: amphibious
Vertical obstacle: 0.5 m
Engine: 2 x ZMZ-4905 petrol
Power output: 2 x 120 hp
Suspension: torsion bar
Armament: 1 x 14.5 mm MG;
1 x 7.62 mm MG
Variants: BTR-70kh, BREM, BTR-70MS, TAB-77

The widely used BTR-70 wheeled APC in parade trim.

At first sight the **BTR-80** resembles the earlier BTR-70 (previous entry) but there are numerous differences. Although not immediately visible the main change is that the previous pair of petrol engines have been replaced by a single V-8 diesel unit producing 210 hp, although later models may have a 260 hp unit. Another change is that entry doors have been added each side to speed up troop entering and leaving, although the doors mean that the number of troops carried is reduced to seven, although in greater comfort than on earlier models. The one-man turret has also been modified to allow the 14.5 mm heavy MG barrel to be fully elevated to engage aircraft and helicopters. There are many other detail changes on the **BTR-80** series, including NBC agent sensor equipment to close the vehicle down automatically in the event of an NBC attack.

There is a specialised NBC reconnaissance variant of the **BTR-80,** known as the RkHM-4-01, fitted with specialised sensing, classification and warning equipment.

Another **BTR-80** variant is a command vehicle while the 2S23 self-propelled gun is a rather more involved model mounting a high-elevation 120 mm breech-loading mortar in an enlarged fully-traversable turret - the exact status of this model is uncertain but it has been offered for export sales.

The latest in the series to date is the **BTR-80A** which converts the usual APC into a wheeled IFV. First shown in late 1994, the **BTR-80A** has yet to leave the prototype stage but has already been promoted for export sales with at least two engine pack options.

On the **BTR-80A** the turret is replaced by an external weapon station mounting a potent 30 mm cannon plus a 7.62 mm MG; the vehicle crew remains at two but the number of troops carried is eight. The weight of this model is increased to 14.55 tonnes but it remains fully amphibious, in common with all the other wheeled BTR series vehicles.

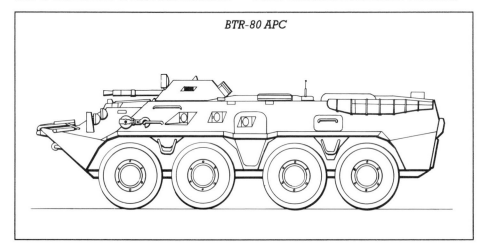

BTR-80 APC

Specification

Crew: 3
Seating: 7
Weight: (combat) 13,600 kg
Length: 7.65 m
Width: 2.9 m
Height: 2.35 m
Ground clearance: 0.475 m
Track: 2.41 m
Max speed: (road) 80 km/h
Fuel capacity: 290 litres
Range: up to 600 km
Fording: amphibious
Vertical obstacle: 0.5 m
Engine: V-8 diesel
Power output: 210 hp (poss 260 hp)
Suspension: torsion bar
Armament: 1 x 14.5 mm MG;
1 x 7.62 mm MG
Variants: BTR-80A IFV, 2S23, RKhM-4-01 -
see also text

The external 30 mm cannon marks this BTR-80 model as the BTR-80A.

MT-LB Carrier   Former Soviet Union

The **MT-LB** is not really an APC but an amphibious multi-purpose tracked carrier which may be adapted to meet virtually any armoured support vehicle requirement conceivable, for its simple basic design has proved to be highly adaptable.

First seen in 1970, the **MT-LB** was originally employed as an artillery tractor but is now only rarely encountered in this role. Instead, the **MT-LB** can carry up to 11 troops in its main load-carrying compartment behind the two-man crew compartment, which may be surmounted by a 7.62 mm MG in a small turret for the commander. However, the **MT-LB** can function as a front line load carrier for anything from ammunition to fuel, or as a mobile platform for numerous weapon systems and even as the basis for a self-propelled 122 mm howitzer (the 2S9). One variant, the **MT-LBV,** has extra-wide tracks for operations over snow and soft terrain.

There are also light repair and recovery variants, 82 and 120 mm

mortar carriers, combat engineer reconnaissance vehicles, battlefield radar carriers, armoured ambulances, air defence missile carriers, the seemingly inevitable command posts for all roles, NBC reconnaissance vehicles, and so on - the list seems endless and probably is.

Just one series of examples may suffice. In 1993 Sweden purchased some 800 former East German **MT-LB** carriers (at a very favourable price). Some of these will be modernised, with about 200 being stripped down for

spares. Once updated these will be used by the Swedish Army as command vehicles, load carriers, and to carry mortars and other weapons. Swedish expertise has also been employed to mount a 40 mm Bofors Gun turret on a Polish licence-produced **MT-LB** chassis, possibly for Polish Army service.

MT-LBs have also been licence-produced in Bulgaria; their BMP-23 IFV is based on the **MT-LB** and they have developed their own array of variants.

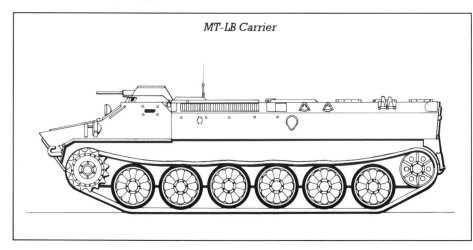

MT-LB Carrier

Specification

Crew: 2
Seating: up to 11
Weight: (combat) 11,900 kg
Length: 6.454 m
Width: 2.86 m
Height: 1.865 m
Ground clearance: 0.4 m
Track: 2.3 m
Max speed: (road) 61.5 km/h
Fuel capacity: 450 litres
Range: 500 km
Fording: amphibious
Vertical obstacle: 0.6 m
Engine: YaMZ 238 V V-8 diesel
Power output: 240 hp
Suspension: torsion bar
Armament: 1 x 7.62 mm MG
Variants: Many - see text

A captured Iraqi Army MT-LB APC, a versatile and much-used general purpose carrier.

55

For various reasons, when most Warsaw Pact nations adopted the BTR-60P series of wheeled APCs (qv) in the early 1960s Poland and Czechoslovakia decided to jointly develop their own equivalent.

The result entered service in 1964 and was known as the **SKOT**, labelled in the West as the OT-64 APC. Using many components from the TATRA 813 series of high mobility trucks, the **SKOT** was jointly produced, the chassis and main components in Czechoslovakia and the armoured hull and other parts in Poland. In overall layout the **SKOT** series resembles the BTR-60P series but the two types are very different, the fully amphibious **SKOT** being bulkier overall and having, for instance, large entry doors in the hull rear while the later models have the turret mounted in the centre of the hull roof. This turret was not installed on early production models which were armed only by a single pintle-mounted 7.62 mm MG.

The turret was added to the **SKOT-2,** used mainly by Poland,

mounting a 7.62 or 12.7 mm MG. The **SKOT-2A** became the main production variant, with the main turret armament being uprated to a 14.5 mm MG capable of high elevation angles.

The **SKOT-2AP** had a revised turret outlines and some export models also had alternative turret outlines.

Other **SKOT** variants included command and radio vehicles, a mobile front line workshop, and a Polish combat engineer vehicle.

As well as being used by Czechoslovakia and Poland the **SKOT** series was also exported in significant numbers to several nations such as Morocco, India, Cambodia, the Sudan and Iraq (among others); Hungary was another Warsaw Pact user. With many of these nations the **SKOT** series is no longer employed as a front line vehicle but is instead issued to police and other internal security forces.

At one time **SKOT** APCs were often deployed carrying ATGW but this is now rarely seen.

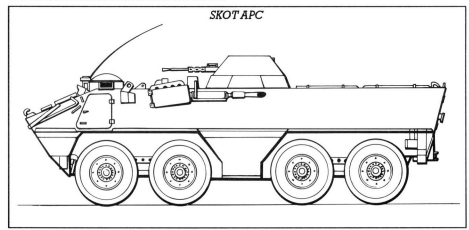

SKOT APC

Specification:

Crew: 2
Seating: 18
Weight: (combat) 14,300 kg
Length: 7.44 m
Width: 2.55 m
Height: (hull top) 2.06 m
Ground clearance: 0.46 m
Track: 1.86 m
Max speed: (road) 94 km/h
Fuel capacity: 320 litres
Range: 710 km
Fording: amphibious
Vertical obstacle: 0.5 m
Engine: TATRA 928-14 V-8 diesel
Power output: 180 hp
Suspension: springs and shock absorbers
Armament: 1 x 7.62 mm MG
Variants: SKOT, SKOT-2, SKOT-2A, SKOT-2AP - also, see text

The large and bulky SKOT (OT-64) APC, seen here in Czech Army service.

Fahd APC   Egypt

The **Fahd** wheeled APC was developed in response to an Egyptian Army requirement by Thyssen Henschel of Germany with the prototypes being manufactured in Germany. Thereafter production switched to state-owned factories in Egypt, from 1985 onwards, where the **Fahd** gradually replaced a whole host of older APC types in service.

The **Fahd** is essentially a box-type armoured steel body built onto the chassis of a Mercedes-Benz 1117/32 4 x 4 truck, with extensive use being made of readily available commercial components, where possible.

The large body is highly amenable to alteration for a number of purposes so, apart from the basic APC carrying ten troops who enter through a door at the rear, the **Fahd** can be adapted to become a police or internal security vehicle or act as a minelaying vehicle with banks of mine dispenser tubes installed on a flat bed rear body.

As an APC the **Fahd** is well provided with vision devices for the occupants and air conditioning is standard, as is a central tyre inflation system to allow the vehicle to cross sand and other soft terrain. The roof can be used to mount various types and sizes of turret armed with weapons from 7.62 mm MG up to 20 mm cannon.

One turret conversion changes the **Fahd** into a potential IFV. This is the **Fahd** 30 which involves the complete turret and armament of the BMP-2 IFV (qv). First announced in 1990, the Fahd 30 turret comes complete with roof-mounted ATGW. The basic **Fahd** has been exported, often in an internal security (IS) configuration, with customers including Algeria and Kuwait (both IS), Oman and Zaire.

The vehicles delivered to Kuwait were captured by Iraq during their invasion so their present status is uncertain.

Development of the **Fahd** continues, future variants could include command vehicles, armoured ambulances, specialised missile carriers and recovery vehicles.

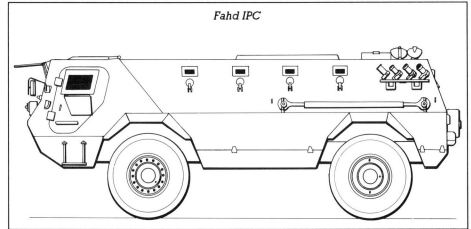

Fahd IPC

Specification

Crew: 2
Seating: up to 10
Weight: (combat) 10,900 kg
Length: 6 m
Width: 2.45 m
Height: 2.45 m
Ground clearance: 0.37 m
Track: not known
Max speed: (road) 90 km/h
Fuel capacity: not known
Range: 800 km
Fording: 0.7 m
Vertical obstacle: 0.5 m
Engine: Mercedes-Benz OM 352A diesel
Power output: 168 hp
Suspension: springs and shock absorbers
Armament: variable- see text
Variants: Fahd 30

One of the many variants of the Fahd APC, seen here armed with a 20 mm cannon turret

APC to IFV

It was the Soviets who introduced the first large-scale employment of the infantry fighting vehicle (IFV).

From the outset, early APCs such as half-tracks carried a variety of weapons, usually machine guns, to enable their occupants to at least defend themselves against potential attackers; these measures were primarily defensive. In general the early APCs had to depend on supporting arms such as tanks and artillery to cover their movements. Fire support by APCs for other APCs was very limited. Even with the 1950s generation of APCs little was changed. What weapons were carried were usually served by crew or infantry squad members having to expose themselves to incoming fire and artillery bursts through an open hatch or cupola to operate whatever weapon was involved. But once that weapon was protected within a turret the potential of what was to become the IFV was realised.

The gun turret was not the only firepower amplifier on the IFV. Even before viable gun turrets appeared anti-tank guided weapons (ATGW) or recoilless rifles were often fired from open APC roof hatches. The missiles involved were usually those normally carried by the infantry passengers but with the advent of the IFV more powerful and longer range ATGWs appeared, a typical example from the West being the American wire-guided TOW series.

On the IFV the launchers for such ATGWs were often specialised turrets but the latest generation of IFVs now have their ATGW launchers as adjuncts to gun turrets to provide greater variety of support firepower for the infantry - the specialised ATGW turrets have instead converted some IFV variants into specialised tank killers.

Thus by the late 1970s the APC had become the father to the IFV. But even before then, during the 1960s, a series of projects in which APCs assumed combat turrets with cannon-type weapons had appeared.

The old APC thus became less of a personnel carrier and more of a combat vehicle capable of producing its own fire support on the move and of operating in unison with other similarly-armed vehicles to attack or defend objectives.

The number of combat roles for the old infantry carriers began to expand. From being a simple armoured 'battlefield taxi' the personnel carrier began to assume patrolling, surveillance and reconnaissance roles plus, as it carried a viable weapon, the ability to engage similar enemy vehicles and remove them and their precious cargoes from the battlefield.

Protection for the occupants and crew expanded to incorporate collective chemical and nuclear warfare protection systems while more consideration was given to protecting vehicle occupants against land mine detonations. The relatively low cost APC had become the far more costly IFV.

Opposite: British troops training on a *Warrior* IFV.

APC to IFV (cont.)

If there was one vehicle that marked the complete transition from APC to IFV it was the Soviet BMP-1. When the BMP-1 appeared other IFVs such as the British MCV-80 (now the Warrior), the German Marder 1 and the American M2/M3 Bradley IFVs, were already in the pipeline but the appearance of the well-armed, well-protected and agile BMP-1 accelerated their development processes.

Combat experience in Afghanistan was to demonstrate that the BMP-1 design had its limitations, especially in the 73 mm low velocity gun armament, so it was gradually supplemented by the BMP-2 with its more versatile 30 mm cannon. Eventually the formidable BMP-3 appeared, but today the latest Bradleys, Warriors, Pandurs and many other Western IFVs are on a technical and firepower parity with the ex-Soviet APC/IFV fleets that once seemed such a formidable challenge.

Above: *The Saxon wheeled APC.*

Opposite: *Not all APCs and IFVs are destined for the front line. This Renault VAB 6 x 6 is destined for an internal security role.*

SISU XA-180 APC   Finland

In 1982 the Finnish government carried out a series of trials to select a replacement APC for their ageing BTR-60P APCs (qv). The design selected was the **SISU XA-180**, ordered at the end of 1983 and entering production soon after.

The **XA-180** is based on the SISU SA-150 6 x 6 truck and uses many identical components, although the **XA-180**'s chassis and 6 x 6 wheelbase arrangement is very different. The layout of the **XA-180** is somewhat unusual with the engine located just behind the driver on the left-hand side with the troop compartment at the rear - troops enter and leave via two doors in the hull rear.

Early **XA-180**s were unarmed but this was later rectified when a 12.7 mm MG on a ring type mounting was added.

XA-180s intended for United Nations support missions (as many are) may have a twin 12.7 mm MG mounting while others have small turrets. At first all production of the **XA-180** was for the Finnish armed forces but since the type proved ideal for operations with United Nations forces **XA-180**s have also been produced for Norwegian, Austrian, Irish and Swedish troops operating in locations such as the Lebanon and Bosnia.

The original **XA-180** has now been replaced in production by the XA-185 which features an uprated engine (246 hp), a revised roof hatch layout, and new axles which impart a slightly higher silhouette.

One XA-185 variant, the XA-186, is operated by Norwegian United Nations troops in Bosnia, carrying a twin 12.7 mm MG turret. The Finnish Army operates a small number of **XA-180**s fitted with folding hydraulic masts which lift air defence radar scanners above the tree line to provide an all-round search pattern.

Another variant, the XA-181, has been converted to carry the Crotale air defence missile system - the Finnish Army has about 20 of these.

Production of the XA-185 continues.

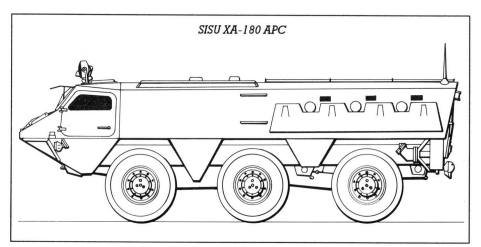

SISU XA-180 APC

Specification

Crew: 2
Seating: 10
Weight: (combat) 15,500 kg
Length: 7.35 m
Width: 2.9 m
Height: 2.3 m
Ground clearance: 0.4 m
Track: 2.2 m
Max speed: (road) 100 km/h
Fuel capacity: approx 250 litres (est)
Range: 800 km
Fording: amphibious
Vertical obstacle: 0.5 m

Engine: Valmet diesel
Power output: 236 hp
Suspension: leaf spring and shock absorbers
Armament: 1 x 12.7 mm MG
Variants: XA-181, XA-185, XA-186 -also, see text

The SISU XA-180, Finland's own wheeled APC.

AMX-10P IFV

France

The **AMX-10P** tracked APC was developed for the French Army from 1965 onwards and has since been widely exported; production commenced in 1972. Production ceased in early 1994, by which time some 1,750 had been produced. Most of the production run was for the French Army, the standard **AMX-10P** vehicle being armed with a 20 mm cannon in a two-man turret.

The eight troop occupants are seated in a compartment at the rear, entering and leaving via a wide power-operated ramp in the back of the hull.

The vehicle is fully amphibious, being propelled in the water by two water jet units in the hull rear.

One variant, the AMX-10 HOT used by Saudi Arabia, has the main armament replaced by a bank of HOT ATGW while on another, the AMX-10 PAC 90 is intended to be a fire support vehicle as it mounts a 90 mm gun. The latter was developed primarily for export sales and was sold to Indonesia and Singapore; Singapore has also procured a version

with a smaller turret mounting a 25 mm cannon.

Variants of the **AMX-10P** abound, many of them having been produced only for trials purposes but several variants have been adopted. One is an unarmed armoured ambulance while another is the AMX-10 ECH repair vehicle. There is a turretless driver training variant and the AMX-10 PC command vehicle.

Others include the AMX-10 SAO and VAO which are intended for forward artillery observation, with the

AMX-10 SAT for artillery survey. The AMX-10 TM tows a 120 mm mortar and carries the crew, plus some ammunition; this variant retains the 20 mm cannon.

One type of **AMX-10P** carries a battlefield surveillance radar. Customers not already mentioned for the **AMX-10** series of vehicles include the United Arab Emirates, Greece, Iraq and Qatar.

An updating package including a more powerful engine is being offered to extend the service life of this series.

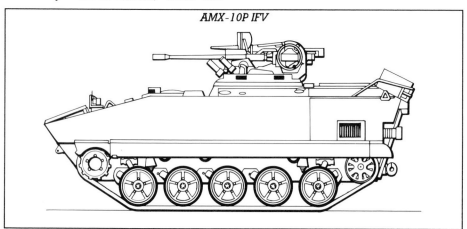

AMX-10P IFV

Specification

Crew: 3
Seating: 8
Weight: (combat) approx 14,500 kg
Length: 5.778 m
Width: 2.78 m
Height: (hull top) 1.92 m
Ground clearance: 0.45 m
Track: approx 2.5 m
Max speed: (road) 65 km/h
Fuel capacity: 525 litres
Range: 600 km
Fording: amphibious
Vertical obstacle: 0.7 m
Engine: Hispano-Suiza HS 115 V-8 diesel
Power output: 300 hp
Suspension: torsion bar
Armament: 1 x 20 mm cannon;
1 x 7.62 mm MG
Variants: AMX-10P HOT, AMX-10P PAC
90, etc - also, see text

The AMX-10P IFV armed with an externally-mounted 20 mm cannon.

67

AMX VCI IFV

The **AMX VCI** was one of the first combat vehicles to enter the IFV category for it was developed during the 1950s, with production commencing during 1957; well over 3,400 were produced, many for export to at least 15 countries, including Argentina where the type was assembled locally.

The **AMX VCI** was developed using the tracked suspension and chassis of the AMX-13 light tank onto which was mounted an armoured superstructure for the three-man crew and up to ten fully equipped troops.

Access to the troop compartment is via two rear hull doors although there are also roof hatches provided. Initially the main armament was a single 7.5 mm MG but over the years this was gradually replaced by a 7.62 or 12.7 mm MG and eventually many vehicles received a 20 mm cannon. All weapons are mounted over the commander's hatch, sometimes in a small turret.

The **AMX VCI** has now been largely withdrawn from service as an IFV, although many armed forces retain them as reserve vehicles. The usual current role of the type is as a support vehicle or carrier for numerous variants have been produced, many of them for trials or as marketing projects.

One of the many models retained by the French Army is the VTT/TB armoured ambulance while the VTT/PC is a command vehicle. The VTT/Cargo can carry up to 3 tonnes of front line stores while the VTT/PM can carry 81 or 120 mm mortars. Numerous sub-variants are used for artillery fire control purposes (VTT/LT), while the VTT/VCA is used to support 155 mm artillery batteries by carrying gun crews and ammunition.

Other vehicles carry RATAC battlefield surveillance radars. This list is not complete and future variants, such as a minelayer with a flat bed rear carrying mine dispenser tubes, can be anticipated.

There is also a programme to re-engine older vehicles to prolong their service lives.

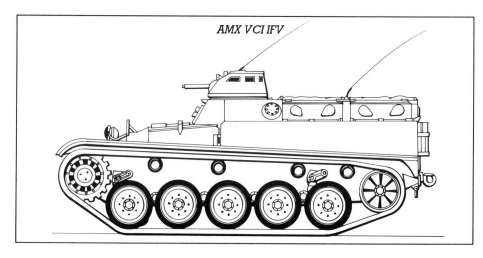
AMX VCI IFV

Specification

Crew: 3
Seating: 10
Weight: (combat) approx 15,000 kg
Length: 5.7 m
Width: 2.67 m
Height: (hull top) 2.1 m
Ground clearance: 0.48 m
Track: 2.16 m
Max speed: (road) 64 km/h
Fuel capacity: 410 litres
Range: up to 550 km
Fording: 1 m
Vertical obstacle: 0.65 m
Engine: Baudouin 6F 11 SRY diesel
Power output: 280 hp
Suspension: torsion bar
Armament: 1 x 20 mm cannon; see text

Variants: See text

The AMX VCI APC, now phased out of French Army service but retained in widespread service elsewhere.

Renault VAB APC

France

The **VAB** was developed by the Saviem/Renault Group to meet a French Army requirement, with production starting in 1976. Since then the **VAB** series has become one of the most diverse of all current French combat vehicles, having been produced with many variations, not the least being the existence of both 4 x 4 and 6 x 6 drive configurations although the two have many components in common. By mid-1994 over 5,000 had been produced, over 4,000 of them for the French armed forces with the rest going to at least ten customer nations, with other undisclosed orders having been placed at one time or another; production still continues. The base model is the 4 x 4 **VAB VTT** APC which carries up to ten troops in the relatively spacious armoured hull.

Most **VAB**s carry at least a 7.62 mm MG although 12.7 mm MGs and 20 mm cannon, with or without the ballistic protection provided by various types of turret, are alternatives. The **VAB** is often allocated to French Army units as an anti-tank vehicle armed with either MILAN or Mephisto ATGW. These vehicles have roof-mounted launcher turrets and carry reload missiles inside the troop compartment; TOW ATGW carriers have been developed.

Other **VAB**s are employed by the French Army for just about every support vehicle function that can be devised. The list includes the usual command vehicle and ambulance, but extends to combat engineer support carrier, communications of all types, 81 mm mortar carrier, 120 mm mortar tractor (with the crews inside the vehicle), surveillance radar platform, electronic warfare (EW), recovery, repair and workshop, and even NBC reconnaissance; many other variants exist, including air defence platforms for guns and missiles, most of them having been produced for export customers.

Internal security models have been produced for home and export sales.

Renault have produced a **VAB** New Generation model featuring numerous design updates and enhancements which can be retrofitted to existing models; to date none have been produced in quantity.

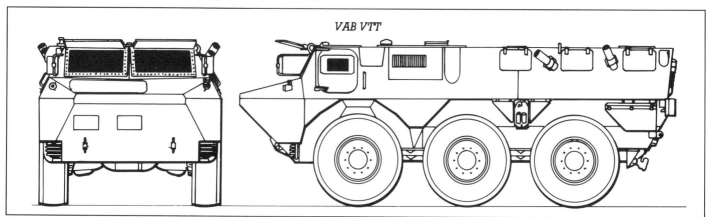

VAB VTT

The 4 x 4 version of the VAB APC, seen here during an amphibious exercise.

Specification

(4 x 4 version)
Crew: 2
Seating: 10
Weight: (combat) approx 13,000 kg
Length: 5.98 m
Width: 2.49 m
Height: (hull top) 2.06 m
Ground clearance: 0.4 m
Track: 2.035 m
Max speed: (road) 92 km/h
Fuel capacity: 300 litres
Range: 1,000 km
Fording: amphibious
Vertical obstacle: 0.5 m
Engine: Renault MIDS 06-20-45 diesel
Power output: 220 hp
Suspension: independent, torsion bar
Armament: See text
Variants: Many - see text

Panhard VCR-TT APC

France

The **Panhard VCR-TT** was developed purely as a commercial venture to provide a relatively low cost and unsophisticated wheeled APC that would meet the requirements of many overseas nations.

It was first shown in 1977 and since then has gained a steady stream of orders to the extent that production on request is still available.

The base model is a 6 x 6 vehicle although a 4 x 4 model is also offered. The latter has been produced in smaller numbers than the 6 x 6 and is virtually a shortened 6 x 6 with the central axle removed; the only known customer to date has been Argentina.

On the 6 x 6 **VCR-TT** the central axle can be raised when the vehicle is travelling along roads. The overall silhouette is quite high, due mainly to the need for headroom for the ten passengers and three crew. Access for the troop compartment is through the rear hull, with the occupants seated on inward-facing benches. The vehicle commander controls the main armament which is usually a 7.62 mm MG over his hatch; a 20 mm cannon or a 60 mm breech-loading mortar are alternatives.

In common with many other APCs the **VCR-TT** is amphibious but there are no water jet units as once in the water propulsion and steering are both carried out via the road wheels.

The spacious rear compartment can be equipped for many applications. VCR variants include mobile workshops for front line repairs, the usual ambulance and command vehicles, plus mobile medical aid posts, air defence missile vehicles (yet to enter production) and anti-tank missile carriers.

From mid-1983 onwards all VCR series vehicles were produced with slightly revised wheelbase dimensions and a lengthened hull. Vehicles sold to Abu Dhabi have a widened hull.

Other customers have included Iraq and Mexico (two command vehicles). Many of the Iraqi vehicles were destroyed during the 1991 Gulf campaign.

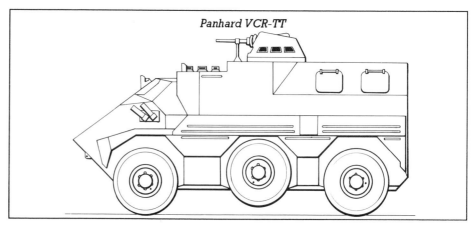

Panhard VCR-TT

Side-on view of a Panhard VCR TT APC - note the raised centre wheels.

Specification
(6 x 6 model)

Crew: 3
Seating: 9
Weight: (combat) 7,900 kg
Length: 4.875 m
Width: 2.5 m
Height: (hull top) 2.13 m
Ground clearance: 0.375 m
Track: 2.115 m
Max speed: (road) 90 km/h
Fuel capacity: 242 litres
Range: 700 km
Fording: amphibious
Vertical obstacle: 0.8 m
Engine: Peugeot PRV V-6 petrol
Power output: 145 hp
Suspension: independent
Armament: 1 x 20 mm cannon or 1 x 7.62 mm MG
Variants: See text

Panhard M3 APC   France

The **Panhard M3** wheeled APC is another French armoured vehicle which was produced primarily as a private venture with the objective being export sales.

With the **M3,** Panhard produced a winner for the **M3** was sold to some 26 known countries, with a final production total of over 1,000. Many of the 4 x 4 drive and other components are identical to those of the Panhard AML series of light armoured cars of which thousands were produced, so adapting that design for the APC market involved mainly the introduction of an sloping-walled armoured box hull plus its interior, and little else. The result was a simple, rugged and adaptable vehicle which has continued to serve many users well ever since production started during 1971.

The **Panhard M3** underwent some detail changes since then but the overall design remained basically unchanged, being little more than an armoured troop carrier with only limited armament, usually a 7.62 mm MG in a small roof-mounted turret or with the weapon on a pintle over a hatch; a 12.7 mm MG or a 20 mm cannon can be installed but this is apparently rarely done.

The ten occupants are provided with access doors in the sides and rear and roof hatches are provided; there are also firing hatches along each side. In addition to the two-man crew and ten passengers it is also possible to carry loads of supplies weighing over 1 tonne.

Variants have been produced, one being an air defence vehicle (M3/VDA) with twin 20 mm cannon and a radar-based fire control system.

There is also the M3/VTS ambulance, the M3/VLA combat engineer vehicle, the M3/VPC mobile command centre, and the M3/VAT repair vehicle.

The **Panhard M3** has also been used to carry battlefield radars.

Production of the **Panhard M3** has now ceased in favour of the Panhard Buffalo (following entry).

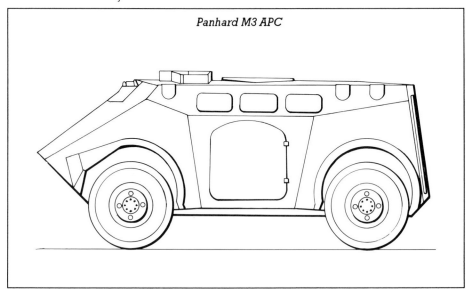

Panhard M3 APC

Specification

Crew: 2
Seating: 10
Weight: (combat) kg
Length: 4.45 m
Width: 2.4 m
Height: (hull top) 2 m
Ground clearance: 0.35 m
Track: 2.05 m
Max speed: (road) 90 km/h
Fuel capacity: 165 litres
Range: 600 km
Fording: amphibious
Vertical obstacle: 0.3 m
Engine: Panhard Model 4 HD petrol
Power output: 90 hp
Suspension: independent, coil spring
Armament: various - see text
Variants: M3/VDA, M3/VDS, M3/VLA, M3/VPC/ M3/VAT

Typical example of a Panhard M3 wheeled APC.

Panhard Buffalo APC   France

The **Panhard Buffalo** wheeled APC was introduced in mid 1985 and replaced the Panhard M3 in production (see previous entry). It is another Panhard private venture aimed at export markets and is basically a revised and updated Panhard M3. The hull is slightly longer and has a revised outline, the wheelbase is increased and there is the option of installing either a Peugeot petrol or diesel engine.

As an APC the **Buffalo** follows the same overall form and layout as the M3 and although some of the internal details remain much the same many have been revised in order to utilise M3 experience and retain component compatibility with other vehicles in the current Panhard armoured vehicle range.

Thus the troop compartment firing and roof hatches are retained virtually unchanged but the side access doors have been enlarged and are better protected.

The commanders station can accommodate a variety of weapon mountings but most examples observed to date involve a 7.62 mm MG. The front of the vehicle can be used to mount a hydraulically-operated dozer blade, either for obstacle-clearing internal security (IS) duties or as an accessory for the combat engineer carrier role. Many other extras could be carried for the IS role, such as smoke projectors and extra shields for the crew and their vision devices.

Other proposed **Buffalo** variants (some of which have been produced in small numbers to date) include a command vehicle with extra radios and other equipment, an 81 mm mortar carrier, a recovery and repair vehicle with a light recovery jib over the hull rear, and an armoured ambulance.

Optional equipment for all models includes a front-mounted winch and air conditioning.

To date **Panhard Buffalos** have been procured by Benin, Columbia and Rwanda, although the current status of the latter is uncertain.

Production continues on request.

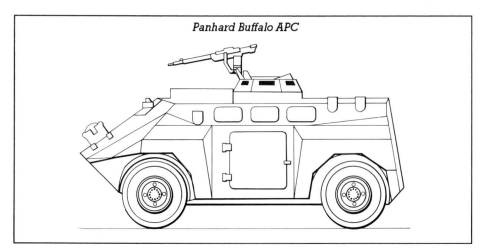

Panhard Buffalo APC

Specification

Crew: 2
Seating: 10
Weight: (combat) 6,600 kg
Length: 4.585 m
Width: 2.4 m
Height: 2 m
Ground clearance: 0.33 m
Track: 2.06 m
Max speed: (road) 90 km/h
Fuel capacity: variable
Range: up to 600 km
Fording: amphibious
Vertical obstacle: 0.4 m
Engine: Peugeot PRV V-6 petrol
Power output: 145 hp
Suspension: independent, coil and spring
Armament: 1 x 7.62 mm MG
Variants: See text

The Panhard Buffalo APC, showing its resemblance to the Panhard M3 from which it was developed.

Transportpanzer 1 Fuchs APC   Germany

The **Transportpanzer 1**, or Fuchs (Fox) as it is known, was developed to be an armoured amphibious load carrier utilising commercially available components wherever possible. Following extensive trials with prototype vehicles the main production run was carried out by Thyssen Henschel from 1979 onwards, with production still continuing. From its origins as a load carrier the fully amphibious **Transportpanzer 1** has been modified to meet many other requirements, one being as an APC capable of carrying up to 14 troops seated individually in the load compartment (the German Army limits the number of troops carried to ten). As a load carrier the vehicle can carry nearly 3 tonnes of

supplies under armour, with this version being convertible to an armoured ambulance when necessary. However, the **Transportpanzer 1** has been adapted for many other purposes. The German Army alone uses the **Transportpanzer 1** as a RASIT battlefield surveillance radar carrier, combat engineer carrier, electronic warfare vehicle (without the amphibious capability), command and communications centre, an explosive ordnance disposal vehicle for the German Air Force, and an NBC reconnaissance vehicle. Other nations use the latter variant, including Israel, the United Kingdom, and the United States.

The US Army has adopted the NBC vehicle as the M93 Fox and expects to

have over 300 examples; most current production is for this version.

Other export variants of the **Transportpanzer 1** include an 81 mm mortar carrier, a 120 mm mortar tractor, a general purpose armoured support vehicle, and an IFV version mounting a 20 or 25 mm cannon in an external mounting on the roof. Customers to date (apart from the NBC version) include Turkey, Saudi Arabia, the Netherlands, and Venezuela. The armament carried varies according to role and user nation. Most carrier versions are limited to a single 7.62 mm machine gun but other models may have various 12.7 mm MG or 20 mm cannon installations in small turrets or external weapon stations.

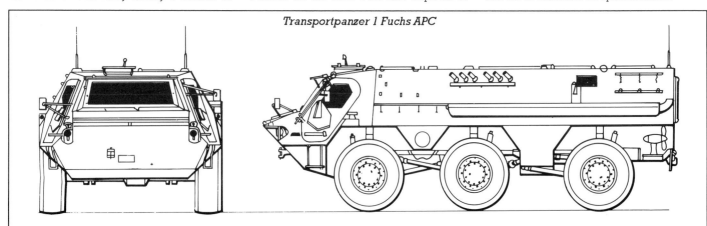

Transportpanzer 1 Fuchs APC

Specification

Crew: 2
Seating: up to 14
Weight: (combat) approx 17,000 kg
Length: 6.83 m
Width: 2.98 m
Height: (hull top) 2.3 m
Ground clearance: 0.406 m
Track: 2.54 m
Max speed: (road) 105 km/h
Fuel capacity: 390 litres
Range: 800 km
Fording: amphibious
Vertical obstacle: 0.6 m
Engine: Mercedes-Benz Model OM 402A
V-8 diesel
Power output: 320 hp
Suspension: independent
Armament: 1 x 20 mm cannon or
1 x 7.62 mm MG
Variants: See text

The Transportpanzer 1 Fuchs seen here in APC form.

Thyssen UR-416   Germany

The first prototype of the **Thyssen UR 416** wheeled APC appeared in 1965 as a private venture project to produce an internal security (IS) vehicle with military applications.

In order to keep down overall costs and provide compatibility with commercial sources of component supply the design was based on the chassis of the Mercedes-Benz Unimog all-terrain truck to which was added a well-sloped armoured steel body; for repairs or maintenance the armoured shell can be lifted directly off the chassis in one piece. The resultant **UR 416** was widely adopted as an internal security vehicle but in some nations it is also issued to the military for various purposes.

Late production versions of the vehicle are known as the **UR 416 M**.

The commander and driver are seated side-by-side, in what would normally have been the truck cab, looking through windscreens which can be covered by armoured shutters when necessary. The eight passengers are seated in the rear, provided with side and rear access doors. For most IS purposes no armament other than smoke projectors is carried but for military missions small turrets mounting one or two 7.62 mm MGs are available; a simple pintle mounting over the roof hatch is an alternative.

Optional equipment includes a front-mounted winch, run-flat tyres, smoke dischargers in either a turret or along the hull sides, air conditioning, and night vision devices. Known variants include a mobile workshop, an ambulance, and the usual command and communications variants. Also available is a patrol and reconnaissance model with an optional turret mounting a 20 mm cannon.

Users of the **UR 416** and **UR 416 M** include, Nigeria, Spain, Turkey, Venezuela, Kenya, South Korea, Morocco, Ecuador, Qatar, Saudi Arabia and Peru - there are other users. In most of these countries the vehicles are used mainly for the IS role.

Production continues as required.

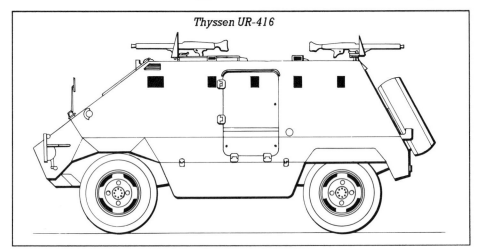
Thyssen UR-416

Specification:

Crew: 2
Seating: 8
Weight: (combat) 7,600 kg
Length: 5.1 m
Width: 2.25 m
Height: 2.25 m
Ground clearance: 0.44 m
Track: 1.78 m
Max speed: (road) 81 km/h
Fuel capacity: 150 litres
Range: up to 700 km
Fording: 1.3 m
Vertical obstacle: 0.55 m
Engine: Mercedes-Benz OM 352 diesel
Power output: 120 hp
Suspension: coil spring
Armament: 1 x 7.62 mm MG (if fitted)
Variants: see text

The UR-416 wheeled APC, basically a Unimog truck chassis with an armoured body.

IFV Tactics

The space and weight demands of gun turrets means that the number of infantry carried by most IFVs is usually far less than the potential capacity of a dedicated APC. However, the reduced numbers of IFV-borne troops can now more than make their presence felt with greater impact due to their potential firepower.

Modern infantry weapons, such as the small calibre assault rifle and light machine gun, can deliver far greater firepower than past generations of small arms so when this potential is coupled with the main armament of the IFV the result is not just greater combat force but the need to rethink infantry tactics.

Infantry still has to take ground and hold it against attack but the way they do so now has altered. Infantry may still have to dismount from IFVs during the final stages of an attack but they do so close to their objective and with the covering fire of their parent IFVs to support them.

During an approach to an objective IFV troops usually have opportunity to utilise their personal weapons through firing ports in the troop compartment walls or exit points. They can accomplish this effectively as they are usually well provided with vision blocks or other devices to observe what is happening outside the confines of their vehicle.

Once an objective has been taken IFVs can be deployed to provide defensive firepower to add to that provided by the infantry, using not just their machine guns or cannon, but the ATGWs which are now an integral part of the armament of any IFV.

One of the current tactical problems for IFV-borne infantry is how to make the best use of all this potential firepower.

Operations no longer involve a headlong rush at an objective and the subsequent dismounted infantry attacks of the APC era. Instead infantry tactics are now very much a matter of firefights, mutual inter-IFV fire and manoeuvre support, and inter-vehicle engagements at long ranges.

Right: Warriors in the advance with a Harrier sweeping overhead.

IFV Tactics (cont.)

It must not be forgotten that IFVs still operate in close proximity to, or in co-operation with, tanks. Thus the old infantry-armour associations and working methods have also come under scrutiny to make the best possible use of their combined shock tactics and firepower.

In a similar manner few armoured operations can take place without artillery support so they too have been drawn into what seem the most routine infantry operations.

The key, as always, is inter-communication to an extent that past foot soldiers would not have dared contemplate.

While such situations are familiar to tank crews, much of this is quite novel to the infantry for whom the only solution is a course of thorough retraining and subsequent experimentation to discover how best to go about their tasks in the future.

Campaigns such as that in the Persian Gulf in 1991, during which IFVs were deployed by the West for the first time on any significant scale, could provide only an inkling of how to proceed.

In a similar manner, during the deployment of BMP-1 IFVs in Afghanistan the changed tactical approaches mechanised infantry commanders now have to adopt were highlighted.

The 1994-1995 close-in fighting in Chechenya provided an indication of how the Russian Army failed to heed those indications.

The future for the infantry seems to indicate more time in gunnery and mission simulators as new skills are assimilated and less time spent in pounding around training areas.

Training armoured combat vehicle personnel is becoming increasingly expensive, so electronic simulators are assuming an ever more important role in training for all tasks from driving and gunnery to inter-vehicle fire command and control.

Above: One of the most advanced IFVs in service, the Swedish CV90.

Below: APC versatility, a Canadian M113 equipped for the combat engineer role.

Thyssen Henschel Condor APC　　　Germany

Having witnessed the sales success of their UR-416 series of vehicles (see previous entry), Thyssen Henschel completed a prototype of their **Condor** APC in 1978. Their UR 416 technique of employing commercial components wherever possible was followed (the **Condor** engine and drive train are also installed on some Unimog all-terrain trucks). The first order, placed by Malaysia and for 459 units, was announced in late 1981. Production has continued ever since, with over 600 vehicles having been manufactured by mid-1994. By comparison with the earlier UR 416 the **Condor** is a much larger and heavier vehicle with a more aggressive appearance. It is also fully amphibious, being propelled in the water by a steerable propeller under the hull. The ballistic protection is also improved and there is more internal space for either troops (up to 12) or supplies. The internal layout has also been revised, with the driver seated well forward next to the engine, which is located on the right-hand side of the hull. The vehicle commander is seated behind the driver, with access through a roof hatch to a weapon station which may be protected by a small turret.

Optional weapon mountings include a 20 mm cannon with a coaxial 7.62 mm MG, while some of the troops carried can fire their personal weapons through weapon ports in the upper hull sides. Some APCs produced for the Malaysian contract have the 20 mm cannon one-man turret. Other models produced for the same order including command vehicles, an ambulance, and a fitter's vehicle provided with a light crane. Other proposed Condor variants include ATGW carriers and models with various types of weapon turret.

Air conditioning is optional on all models, as are a collective NBC system, an intercom, night vision systems and a recovery winch. Apart from the vehicles supplied to Malaysia, **Condor** sales have also been made to Indonesia, Portugal, Turkey, Uruguay and some other undisclosed countries.

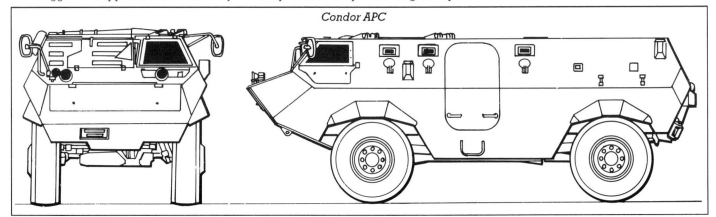

Condor APC

The Condor wheeled APC undergoing
German Army trials.

Specification

Crew: 2
Seating: 12
Weight: (combat) 12,400 kg
Length: 6.13 m
Width: 2.47 m
Height: (hull top) 2.18 m
Ground clearance: 0.475 m
Track: 1.84 m
Max speed: (road) 100 km/h
Fuel capacity: 280 litres
Range: 900 km
Fording: amphibious
Vertical obstacle: 0.55 m
Engine: Mercedes-Benz OM 352 A diesel
Power output: 168 hp
Suspension: coil springs
Armament: 1 x 20 mm cannon;
1 x 7.62 mm MG
Variants: See text

Marder 1 IFV   Germany

The **Marder 1** IFV is based on a special tracked chassis originally developed in the early 1960s to create a common platform for a whole host of armoured vehicles of which an IFV was only one component.

First delivered in 1970, the **Marder 1** was produced by two companies, Rheinstahl and MaK, with final production totals reaching 3,111 in 1975 when manufacture of the IFV ceased. Over the years the **Marder 1** underwent numerous updates, resulting in a Marder 1 A1, then 1 A1A and 1 A2, and finally with 1 A3. All existing models are being modified up to the latter state which involves extra frontal armour, the full provision of night vision devices, changes to roof hatch arrangements, and other details such as the provision of stowage boxes along the sides. Also involved are suspension changes as the latest modifications increased the **Marder 1** A3 weight to some 35 tonnes, making it one of the largest and heaviest of all IFVs (and probably the most expensive) - more enhancement programmes are forecast. Yet the number of troops carried in the troop compartment at the rear is only five or six, even if a MILAN ATGW launcher and reload missiles are included. Even so, **Marder 1** is a formidable vehicle almost resembling a tank but armed with an externally mounted 20 mm cannon and a coaxial 7.62 mm MG over a two-man turret; the hull superstructure armour is well sloped to add protection.

Throughout its life the **Marder 1** has been the basis for several variants but only a few have been accepted for German Army service. One is a Roland air defence system based on the same chassis while another has been converted to carry a battlefield surveillance radar antennae on a rising hydraulic arm.

A driver training tank with the turret replaced by a fixed superstructure for the instructor is in service.

There was a programme to produce a simplified **Marder 1** IFV in Argentina - this is described in a separate section (VCTP - qv).

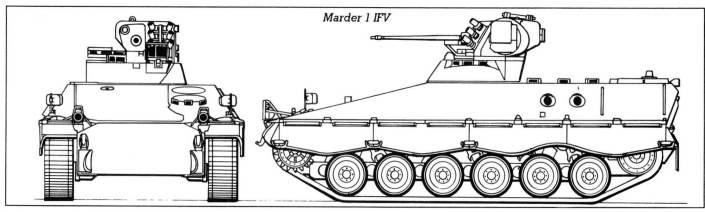

Marder 1 IFV

The heavy Marder 1 A3 IFV, the model with all the latest modifications incorporated.

Specification

(Marder 1 A3)

Crew: 3
Seating: 5 or 6
Weight: (combat) approx 35,000 kg
Length: 6.88 m
Width: 3.38 m
Height: (hull top) 1.9 m
Ground clearance: 0.455 m
Track: 2.62 m
Max speed: (road) 65 km/h
Fuel capacity: 652 litres

Range: 500 km
Fording: with preparation, 2 m
Vertical obstacle: 1 m
Engine: MTU MB 833 Ea-500 diesel
Power output: 600 hp
Suspension: torsion bar
Armament: 1 x 20 mm cannon;
1 x 7.62 mm MG; 1 x MILAN ATGW
Variants: Marder 1 A1, 1 A1A, 1 A2, 1 A3

VCC-80 IFV

The **VCC-80** tracked IFV is a joint development by IVECO and the former OTO Melara (now OTOBREDA) to produce an IFV to meet an Italian Army requirement. To date three prototypes have been produced and the programme awaits further funding but it provides an example of the development path that future IFVs are taking.

The **VCC-80** is a true IFV, having a powerful 25 mm Oerlikon-Contraves cannon mounted in an electrically-operated two-man turret. This cannon is provided with an advanced fire control system of a type more commonly associated with MBTs as it involves a laser rangefinder and thermal imaging equipment. The cannon, which has a maximum effective range of some 2,500 metres, can be elevated sufficiently to allow it to engage aircraft or helicopter targets. It also has a coaxial 7.62 mm MG; another 7.62 mm MG weapon station is provided on top of the turret for air and local defence. It is also possible to mount a MILAN or similar ATGW launcher on the turret roof. The hull is welded aluminium onto which are bolted armoured steel plates - this construction system saves weight. Five firing ports are available for the six troops carried in compartment in the hull rear which is also provided with a power operated ramp for entry and egress; there is also air conditioning and a collective NBC system. In addition to an impressive array of optical vision devices, passive night vision equipment is provided for the crew (driver, commander and gunner).

The **VCC-80** can wade through water obstacles up to 1.5 metres deep without preparation. It has been proposed that the torsion bar suspension installed on the prototypes could be replaced with a more efficient hydropneumatic system on production models. It has also been proposed that the 25 mm cannon could be replaced by an OTOBREDA 60 mm high velocity gun in a special turret on some vehicles.

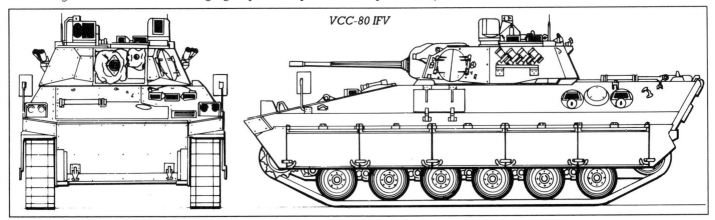

VCC-80 IFV

Specification

Crew: 3
Seating: 6
Weight: (combat) approx 21,700 kg
Length: 6.705 m
Width: 3 m
Height: (hull top) 1.75 m
Ground clearance: 0.4 m
Track: not known
Max speed: (road) 70 km/h
Fuel capacity: not known
Range: 500 km
Fording: 1.5 m
Vertical obstacle: 0.85 m
Engine: IVECO 8260 V-6 diesel
Power output: 520 hp
Suspension: torsion bar
Armament: 1 x 25 mm cannon;
2 x 7.62 mm MG
Variants: None to date

The VCC-80 IFV, yet to enter production.

Fiat 6614 APC   Italy

The **Type 6614** wheeled APC was a joint development between FIAT (now part of IVECO) and OTO Melara (now OTOBREDA) and was designed to meet the requirements of the many military and para-military organisations where some form of mobile armoured protection is required for personnel not necessarily operating under front line conditions.

Thus the **Type 6614** APCs in service with the Italian Air Force are used for airfield patrol while the few issued to the Italian Army are operated by alpine units. Others are employed by various Italian police forces and are equipped accordingly.

The **Type 6614** is basically an armoured hull set on a 4 x 4 chassis which is shared by the Type 6616 armoured car - the two vehicles have many automotive components in common.

The passengers enter via a large powered ramp which covers most of the rear hull wall. Two roof hatches are provided through which mortars can be fired, if required. Once inside, most troop positions are provided with a vision block and a firing port for personal weapons.

The main armament, if fitted, is usually a 12.7 mm MG mounted, sometimes with side protection, over the commander's cupola (which is the same as that fitted to the M113 APC (qv) - a small turret can be fitted if required.

The **Type 6614** is fully amphibious if the need arises with propulsion once in the water provided by the road wheels.

Optional equipment can include a recovery winch, night vision equipment, smoke grenade dischargers and an air-conditioning system.

Export sales were made to Argentina, Peru (ten of which were mortar carriers), Somalia, Tunisia and Venezuela.

When production ceased in Italy 1,160 vehicles had been manufactured.

The **Type 6614** is licence produced in South Korea where it is employed by the South Korean Army. The South Korean APC is known as the KM900, while locally introduced variants, known as the KM901, include an armoured ambulance, mortar carriers and command vehicles.

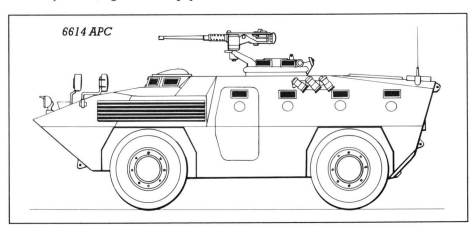

6614 APC

Specification:

Crew: 2
Seating: 9
Weight: (combat) 8,500 kg
Length: 5.86 m
Width: 2.5 m
Height: (hull top) 1.78 m
Ground clearance: 0.37 m
Track: 1.96 m
Max speed: (road) 100 km/h

Fuel capacity: 142 litres
Range: 700 km
Fording: amphibious
Vertical obstacle: 0.4 m
Engine: Model 8062.24 diesel
Power output: 160 hp
Suspension: independent
Armament: 1 x 12.7 mm
Variants: IS, KM900, KM901

The Type 6614 APC used by the Italian Air Force for airfield patrol.

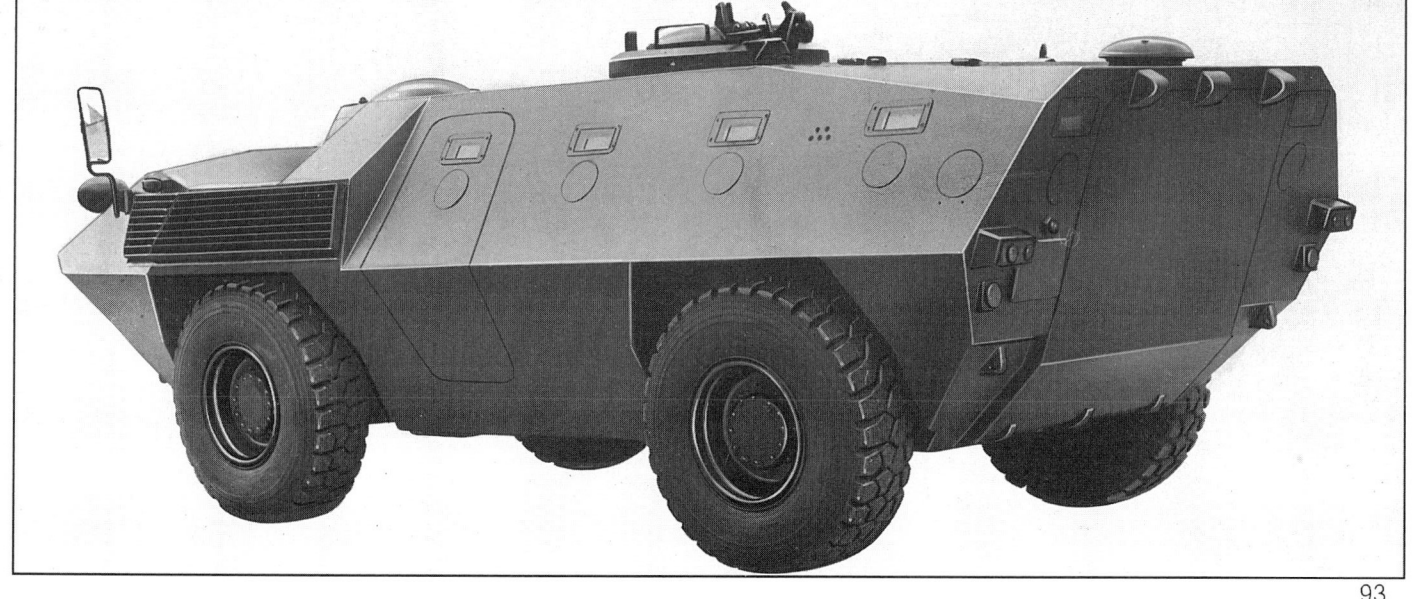

Type 73 AFC

Japan

The requirement for a new APC to supplement the Type SU 60 APC (see following entry) was first issued in early 1967. A lengthy process of test rig and other development then commenced until a Mitsubishi design was selected to become the **Type 73** tracked APC for the Japanese Self-Defence Force.

Production commenced in 1973 with a total of 225 being made; the only users have been the Japanese Self-Defence Force.

The **Type 73** is an entirely conventional tracked APC with a few features all its own, not the least of which is the retention of a forward-firing 7.62 mm bow MG which is operated by a dedicated gunner seated next to the driver. There is also a roof-mounted 12.7 mm Browning MG next to the commander's cupola which is normally manned by one of the nine troops carried; if required this MG can be aimed and fired from within the cover provided by the vehicle's welded aluminium armour. Most of the troops carried have access to firing ports for their personal weapons, two of the ports being in the two outward-opening entry doors in the hull

rear wall.

Passive night vision equipment is provided, as is a collective NBC protection system for all occupants.

The **Type 73** is not normally amphibious unless a special kit, including a trim vane on the front hull and side-slung buoyancy units, has been fitted but not all vehicles have this kit.

The only known direct variant of the **Type 73** is a command vehicle which can be recognised by its raised roof level.

A special variant, the **Type 73** self-propelled wind measuring station, provides meteorological data for 130 mm multiple rocket batteries.

The **Type 73** APC is gradually being replaced by the Type 89 IFV which has a turret-mounted 35 mm cannon, although this is proving to be a slow process. Remaining Type 73s are then destined to become either artillery tractors or converted to become Type 87 tracked ammunition carriers for artillery batteries.

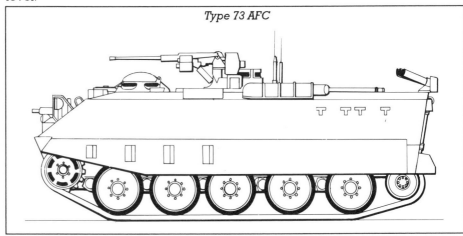

Type 73 AFC

Specification

Crew: 3
Seating: 9
Weight: (combat) 13,300 kg
Length: 5.8 m
Width: 2.8 m
Height: (hull top) 1.7 m
Ground clearance: 0.4 m
Track: 2.56 m
Max speed: (road) 70 km/h
Fuel capacity: 450 litres
Range: 300 km
Fording: amphibious with kit
Vertical obstacle: 0.7 m
Engine: Mitsubishi 4ZF V-4 diesel
Power output: 300 hp
Suspension: torsion bar
Armament: 1 x 12.7 mm MG;
1 x 7.62 mm MG
Variants: Type 75 met. station,
Type 87 ammunition carrier

The Japanese Type 73 APC - note the hull MG.

95

Type SU 60 APC

Japan

Soon after the Japanese Self-Defence Force was established in the 1950s a requirement was placed for a tracked APC; two prototypes were produced. These, and following prototypes, underwent a prolonged period of development before a design was finalised in 1960. Production followed but was slow and fragmented to the extent that the result, the **Type SU 60** APC, can lay claim to being one of the most costly in its category. For all the development work involved, the **Type SU 60** which emerged is still rather underpowered and has limited speed and agility. The vehicle has a crew of four, commander, driver, bow machine gunner and main gunner for the roof-mounted 12.7 mm MG, although the latter may be one of the six troops carried. The interior is rather cramped, there is no provision for the troop compartment occupants to utilise their personal weapons from within the vehicle, and vision to the outside world is limited. No NBC protection system is fitted and the vehicle is not amphibious.

All of these limitations were typical of the time when specialised APCs were still an innovation, and it has to be stated that the **Type SU 60** is still soldiering on with the Japanese Self-Defence Force (no export sales were made or attempted).

A few variants have appeared and remain in service. The Type SV 60 is an 81 mm mortar carrier while the Type SX 60 carries a 4.2-inch (107 mm) rifled mortar, both types having the mortar firing to the rear from inside the troop compartment. Some **Type SU 60s** have been modified to carry two ATGW over the hull rear and a few carry snow-clearing dozer blades.

Prototypes of NBC reconnaissance vehicles based on the **Type SU 60** have been developed but are apparently not yet in widespread service.

The **Type SU 60** APC is destined to be replaced by the Type 89 IFV.

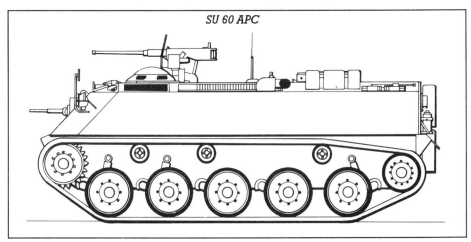

SU 60 APC

Specification

Crew: 4
Seating: 6
Weight: (combat) 11,800 kg
Length: 4.85 m
Width: 2.4 m
Height: (hull top) 1.7 m
Ground clearance: 0.4 m
Track: 2.05 m
Max speed: (road) 45 km/h
Fuel capacity: not known
Range: 230 km
Fording: 1 m
Vertical obstacle: 0.6 m
Engine: Mitsubishi Model 8 HA 21 WT V-8 diesel
Power output: 220 hp
Suspension: torsion bar
Armament: 1 x 12.7 mm MG; 1 x 7.62 mm MG
Variants: Type SV 60, Type SX 60, Type SX 60

Typical of its era in design terms, the Type SU 60 APC.

Korean IFV

The exact designation for the so-called **Korean IFV**, or **KIFV**, has never been disclosed (it may be K-200). It is manufactured by Daewoo Heavy Industries and is based on an American FMC private venture design derived from the M113 APC (qv), although a significant number of local innovations have been introduced; FMC were not involved at any stage.

Aluminium armour from the United Kingdom is used for the hull (covered by spaced laminate steel plates) while the power pack, coupled to an American transmission, is German.

The first **KIFV** examples entered service in 1985, with well over 1,000 units having been manufactured by early 1994. Most have been the IFV version, armed with a pintle-mounted 12.7 mm MG protected by a small open turret behind a shield, plus a 7.62 mm MG over the commander's cupola.

The rear hull roof is raised to increase internal head room for the seven personnel carried; they are provided with an NBC collective protection system as standard.

A trim vane is stowed on the front glacis as the **KIFV** is amphibious, being propelled in the water by its tracks.

The **KIFV** is only one of a family of vehicles on the same base chassis, The others include an air defence vehicle armed with a single 20 mm Vulcan rotary cannon, a recovery vehicle with a prominent recovery crane, an NBC reconnaissance vehicle (which has appeared only in prototype form to date), a command post, an armoured ambulance, two types of mortar carrier (81 mm and 4.2-inch/107 mm), and a tank destroyer carrying a special turret to launch two TOW ATGWs. The latter variant is still at the proposal stage but most of the others are in service with the South Korean armed forces.

More were ordered during 1993 and 1994 by Malaysia for issue to their troops operating with the United Nations forces in the former Yugoslavia.

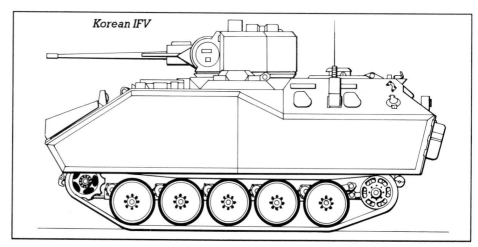

Korean IFV

Specification

Crew: 3
Seating: 7
Weight: (combat) 12,900 kg
Length: 5.486 m
Width: 2.846 m
Height: (hull top, front) 1.829 m
Ground clearance: 0.41 m
Track: approx 2.4 m
Max speed: (road) 74 km/h
Fuel capacity: 400 litres
Range: 480 km
Fording: amphibious
Vertical obstacle: 0.63 m
Engine: MAN D-2848M V-8 diesel
Power output: 280 hp
Suspension: torsion bar
Armament: 1 x 12.7 mm MG;
1 x 7.62 mm MG
Variants: See text

A fully armed Korean IFV with trim vane stowed on front hull.

Ratel IFV   # South Africa

The **Ratel** wheeled IFV is named after the honey badger, noted for its toughness when fighting; many would consider the **Ratel** IFV to be well named. It first appeared in 1974, when sanctions were at their height, having been totally developed within South Africa.

Manufacture was by Sandock-Austral, with final deliveries being made during 1987. All models have a 6 x 6 drive configuration with the long armoured steel hull being specially contoured underneath to minimise land mine damage; if necessary the **Ratel** can travel with two wheels missing. The main variant is the **Ratel 20**, armed with a 20 mm cannon in a two-man turret, plus three 7.62 mm MGs, one coaxial, one over the turret and one on a pintle mounting over a hatch in the rear hull roof. Firing ports and vision devices are provided for most occupants of the crew compartment which is entered through side doors or another at the rear.

A fire support variant, the **Ratel 90**, is virtually identical to the **Ratel 20**

apart from the turret mounting a 90 mm gun and one passenger less to make room for the bulkier ammunition. There is also a **Ratel 60** with a 60 mm breech-loading mortar in the turret.

An anti-tank **Ratel** has a special turret with a bank of three Swift ATGWs over the roof. There is a special command version with a turret with a 12.7 mm MG in a mantlet while an 81 mm mortar carrier does not have a turret at all; the traversable mortar fires through open roof hatches.

Almost any **Ratel** can be rapidly converted into a light ARV by adding a small jib crane to the hull rear.

One of the latest variants is the so-called Enhanced Artillery Observation System (EAOS) on which a raised superstructure behind the drivers position and a special lifting mast carrying a multi-sensor head for target detection and data transmission to a central control post.

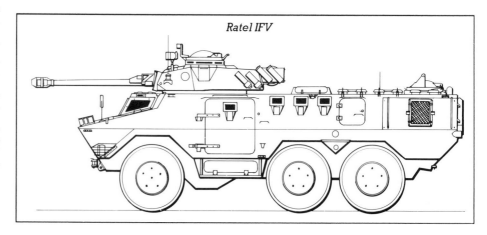

Ratel IFV

Specification

(Ratel 20)
Crew: 2
Seating: 9
Weight: (combat) 18,500 kg
Length: 7.212 m
Width: 2.516 m
Height: (hull top) 2.105 m
Ground clearance: 0.34 m
Track: 2.08 m
Max speed: (road) 105 km/h
Fuel capacity: 430 litres
Range: 1,000 km
Fording: 1.2 m
Vertical obstacle: 0.6 m
Engine: D 3256 BTXF diesel
Power output: 282 hp
Suspension: coil springs
Armament: 1 x 20 mm cannon;
3 x 7.62 mm MG
Variants: Ratel 20, Ratel 60, Ratel 90, Ratel
12.7 Command, Mortar carrier, EAOS,
Swift ATGW

The Ratel 90 IFV armed with a 90 mm main gun.

Casspir APC

The **Casspir** is an unusual vehicle, being in service in much the same form not only with several South African Police forces but also with the South African National Defence Force in a virtually identical form.

Built by TFM (Pty) Limited, the **Casspir** was originally based on a Bedford heavy commercial truck chassis but this was gradually modified and strengthened so that the **Casspir** can be taken as an original design.

The **Casspir** resembles an armoured truck with the armour extending to specially-shaped under-hull plates intended to reduce the effects of land mines and **Casspir** have repeatedly demonstrated that they can indeed survive heavy mine detonations; some have been specially equipped for detecting and clearing mines from roads in remote areas.

The first **Casspir** appeared in 1981. Since then over 2,500 have been produced and many have been rebuilt to extend their service lives, as production has now ceased.

The cab roof has provision for a weapon station, usually a single 7.62 mm MG but police vehicles may have all manner of anti-riot weapons, including a rapid-firing rubber bullet dispenser.

The troops (or police) are seated on outward-facing bench seats down the centre of the rear compartment and are provided with vision blocks and firing ports (police versions usually have larger vision blocks covered by grills). Entry to the rather high off the ground compartment is via a door in the rear - large roof hatches are provided.

Also produced is a **Casspir** ambulance, and three 'specials'. One of these is the Duiker 5000-litre fuel tanker with the tank replacing the troop compartment.

The Blesbock is an armoured load carrier with a cargo body capable of carrying 5 tonnes of supplies - a water tank may form part of the load.

The Gemsbock is a recovery vehicle.

The only known export of **Casspir** was to Peru (20) but several of the states bordering South Africa have acquired examples.

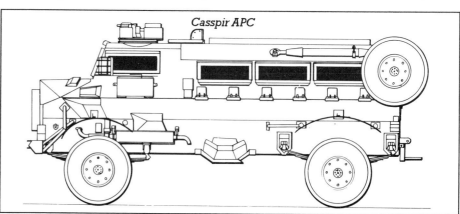

Casspir APC

Specification

Crew: 2
Seating: 10
Weight: (combat) 12,580 kg
Length: 6.87 m
Width: 2.5 m
Height: 2.85 m
Ground clearance: 0.41 m
Track: 2.07 m
Max speed: (road) 90 km/h
Fuel capacity: 220 litres
Range: 850 km

Fording: 1 m
Vertical obstacle: 0.5 m
Engine: ADE 352T diesel
Power output: 170 hp
Suspension: leaf spring
Armament: 1 to 3 7.62 mm MG
Variants: Blesbock, Duiker, Gemsbock

The mine-proofed Casspir wheeled APC, also used as an internal security vehicle.

Mamba APC

At first sight the **Mamba** APC resembles a somewhat bulky but conventional personnel carrier but it was developed not only as an APC but as a mine protected vehicle for operations in areas where land mines are likely to be encountered. It was developed following a long series of mine-proofed vehicles specifically produced to counter the mine warfare conditions once prevalent along the South African borders and in the former Rhodesia.

The **Mamba** produced by Reumech Sandock, thus has an armoured underside with sloped plates intended to direct the worst of a mine blast away from the vehicle. The chassis itself is based around the use of Unimog components and the **Mamba** thus has a remarkable cross country performance.

The steel upper hull can be armoured virtually according to requirements but is usually proof against small arms fire and ammunition splinters. The interior has the commander and driver seated side by side and up to nine troops seated in close proximity in the rear; entry to all position is via a single door at the rear or via roof hatches.

The commander has a roof hatch over which a MG can be mounted, if required. All occupants are provided with bullet-proof windows and the entire roof can be opened up when necessary. The rear area can be readily configured to form an armoured ambulance or a command vehicle.

Other body types include a flatbed body for load carrying, to mount light weapons, or to accommodate a recovery hamper. It has been proposed that the **Mamba** could be fitted out as a VIP protected transport. The **Mamba** has been acquired by the South African National Defence Force and several other countries.

The **Mamba** is also being licence-produced in the United Kingdom by Alvis Limited. The **Mamba** has been trialled by United Nations forces operating in the former Yugoslavia.

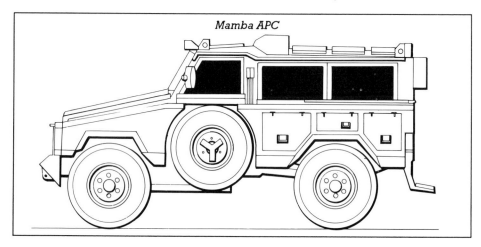

Mamba APC

Specification

Crew: 2
Seating: 9
Weight: (combat) 6,800 kg
Length: 5.46 m
Width: 2.205 m
Height: 2.495 m
Ground clearance: 0.4 m
Track: 1.79 m
Max speed: (road) 102 km/h
Fuel capacity: 200 litres
Range: 900 km
Fording: 1 m
Vertical obstacle: 0.4 m
Engine: Mercedes-Benz OM 352 diesel
Power output: 123 hp
Suspension: coil spring
Armament: 1 x 7.62 mm MG (if fitted)
Variants: See text

The mine-protected Mamba 4 x 4 APC, shown here unarmed.

BMR 3560 50 APC   Spain

The **BMR** series of six-wheeled APCs has been referred to as the **BMR-600** series. It was originally devised during the early 1970s, with the first prototype appearing in 1975. Initial production by various concerns who became the SANTA BARBARA Group commenced in 1979, with the first vehicles being handed over to the Spanish Army the same year.

The **BMR series** has several unusual features, not the least being the independent hydropneumatic suspension which allows the ground clearance to be varied to suit the terrain being traversed.

The hull is welded aluminium, spaced at the front to enhance ballistic protection. The base vehicle, the **BMR 3560.50**, is an APC with a crew of two (the driver and machine gunner/radio operator) plus space for nine troops and the vehicle commander who normally dismounts with the troops via the large power-operated ramp which forms almost the entire rear hull wall. Although the vehicle is amphibious this feature is optional; power once in the water is provided by two water jet units or from the road wheels.

The machine gunner operates a 12.7 mm MG on an external mounting; up to six firing ports are located around the hull.

The **BMR 3560.51** is a command vehicle while the **BMR 3560.53** is a carrier for either an 81 or 120 mm mortar. The **BMR 3560.54** is an armoured ambulance while a more drastic modification forms the **BMR 3560.55** which is an armoured repair and recovery vehicle with a hydraulic crane arm. The **BMR 3560.56** is a radio communications vehicle. The Spanish Army has fitted a 90 mm gun turret to some of their vehicles (**BMR 3564**).

Various types of weapon station have been tested on the **BMR 3560.50** APC. At one time a prototype carrying four HOT ATGWs was rolled out but did not reach the production stage.

Export sales of most production variants have been made to Egypt and Saudi Arabia. Production totals to date are about 1,500 with some 1,000 going to the Spanish armed forces.

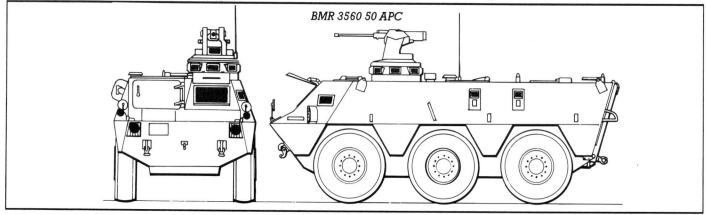

BMR 3560 50 APC

Specification

Crew: 2
Seating: 11
Weight: (combat) approx 14,000 kg
Length: 6.15 m
Width: 2.5 m
Height: (hull top) 2 m
Ground clearance: 0.4 m
Track: 2.08 m
Max speed: (road) 103 km/h
Fuel capacity: 400 litres
Range: 1,000 km
Fording: amphibious
Vertical obstacle: 0.6 m
Engine: Pegaso 9157/8 diesel
Power output: 310 hp
Suspension: independent, hydropneumatic
Armament: 1 x 12.7 mm MG
Variants: BMR 3560.51, 3560.52, 3560.53, 3560.54, BMR 3560.55

Spain's BMR-600 wheeled IFV seen here armed with an externally-mounted 12.7 mm MG.

BLR APC

Spain

The **BLR** wheeled APC was developed to meet numerous Spanish Army requirements for a relatively low cost protected cross country vehicle which could meet various border patrol, internal security (IS) and airport security functions. The **BLR** was developed by the SANTA BARBARA Group under the company designation of **BLR 3545**. The layout of the 4 x 4 BLR differs from most other vehicles of its type in having the engine located centrally at the rear, over the rear axle. Once the occupants have entered via two doors in the hull rear (there are also two side doors, one each side) the interior therefore has a relatively large unimpeded area with space for 12 occupants

plus the driver. Vision blocks are situated along each side wall while the vehicle commander is provided with a centrally-located cupola featuring all-round vision devices. If required, a 7.62 or 12.7 mm MG may be mounted over this cupola, possibly in a small turret; it has been proposed that this weapon station could accommodate heavier weapons, such as 20 or 25 mm cannon or even a 90 mm gun turret, but none has been installed to date.

Special equipment provided for the IS role includes a barricade-clearing device or dozer blade, sirens, loudspeakers, spotlights and smoke or CS agent dischargers. There is also an unusual semi-

automatic system located over each wheel station to extinguish fires. Other optional equipment includes extra radios, run-flat tyres, a front-mounted winch, and night vision devices.

The Spanish Marines operate the **BLR** while more are employed by various Spanish police and para-military forces operating in rural areas. Export sales have been made to Ecuador.

Although no **BLR** variants have been produced to date it has been proposed that the usual command and ambulance models could be readily produced. Production is now as required.

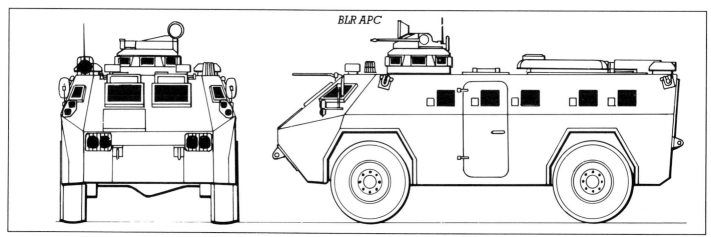

BLR APC

Specification

Crew: 1
Seating: 12
Weight: (combat) 12,000 kg
Length: 5.65 m
Width: 2.5 m
Height: (hull top) 2 m
Ground clearance: 0.32 m
Track: 1.96/2.135 m
Max speed: (road) 93 km/h
Fuel capacity: 200 litres
Range: 570 km
Fording: 1.1 m
Vertical obstacle: 0.3 m

Engine: Pegaso diesel
Power output: 210 hp
Suspension: springs and shock absorbers
Armament: variable - see text
Variants: None to date

*The BLR wheeled APC, frequently deployed
as a general purpose base patrol vehicle.*

Combat Vehicle 90 IFV

Sweden

The **Combat Vehicle 90** (or **CV 90 - Stridsfordon 90** in Swedish) was developed specifically to meet a Swedish Army requirement from the early 1980s onwards, with the first production order being placed in 1991.

The **CV 90**, a joint development by Hagglunds Vehicles AB and Bofors AB, is one of the heaviest armed of all current IFVs with the main armament on the **CV 9040** IFV being a 40 mm Bofors Gun capable of firing potent APFSDS armour-piercing projectiles as well as an array of other ammunition. The gun is mounted in a two-man power-operated turret together with a 7.62 mm coaxial MG; a Bofors BILL ATGW can be mounted over

a hatch in the crew compartment roof. Fire control for the main gun is carried out using a computer-based system employing a laser rangefinder.

Up to eight troops can be carried in the troop compartment at the rear. The **CV 9040** IFV is only one of an extended family of **CV 90** vehicles with most models intended for the Swedish Army. The **CV 9040** AAV is an air defence vehicle, also with a 40 mm Bofors Gun but with an added target-seeking radar on the turret and firing proximity-fuzed ammunition. The **CV 90** FCV (forward command vehicle) and **CV 90** FOV (forward observation vehicle) have their armament limited to a single 7.62 mm MG while the

CV 90 ARV (armoured recovery vehicle) is a turretless hull with a front-mounted anchor/dozer blade and an internal winch.

A **CV 90** MC (mortar carrier) mounting a 120 mm mortar has been proposed but is not yet ordered. Norway has ordered the **CV 9030** IFV with a 30 mm cannon as the main armament.

A private venture model is known as the **CV 90105** tank destroyer, a combination of the **CV 90** chassis and hull with a Giat Industries TML turret mounting a 105 mm high velocity gun; to date only a prototype has been produced and tested.

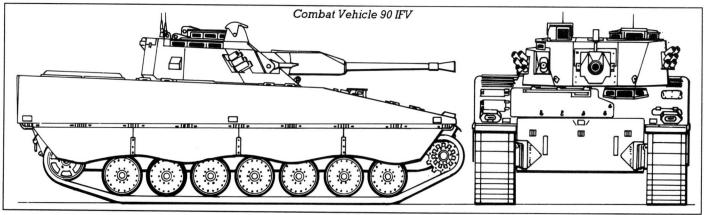

Combat Vehicle 90 IFV

Specification

(CV 9040 IFV)
Crew: 3
Seating: 8
Weight: (combat) 22,400 kg
Length: 6.471 m
Width: 3.01 m
Height: (hull top, front) 1.64 m
Ground clearance: 0.45 m
Track: approx 2.5 m
Max speed: (road) 70 km/h
Fuel capacity: 525 litres
Range: not released
Fording: not released
Vertical obstacle: approx 0.5 m
Engine: Scania DS 14 diesel
Power output: 550 hp
Suspension: torsion bar
Armament: 1 x 40 mm gun;
1 x 7.62 mm MG
Variants: CV 9040 AAV, CV 90 FCV, CV 90 FOV, CV 90 AFV, CV 90 MC, CV 90105

CV-90 IFV armed with a Bofors 40 mm gun as the main armament.

Pansarbandvagn 302 APC   Sweden

The **Pansarbandvagn 302**, or **Pbv 302**, fully tracked amphibious APC was first mooted in 1961 when the then Hagglund and Soner (now Hagglunds Vehicle AB) received a contract to develop such a vehicle. Prototypes appeared during 1962 with production of 700 units commencing the following year.

The **Pbv 302** is operated only by the Swedish armed forces and remains in service with them, having been scheduled for replacement by the CV 90 series (see previous entry).

The base **Pbv 302** APC is typical of its design era, being little more than an armoured steel box set on a tracked chassis. The armour is proof against projectiles up to 20 mm in calibre while the main armament, a magazine-fed 20 mm cannon capable of high elevation to engage aircraft or helicopter targets, is mounted in a small one-man turret off-set to the left of the front hull roof.

The nine troops carried enter through large doors in the hull rear; there is no provision for them to fire their weapons once inside the hull other than from the open hydraulically-operated roof hatches; they also lack vision devices once the hatches are closed down.

After a front-mounted trim vane has been raised the **Pbv 302** is fully amphibious, being propelled in the water by its tracks.

Direct **Pbv 302** variants include a command vehicle (Stripbv 3021), and two artillery fire control or direction vehicles (Epbv 3022 and Bpipbv 3023).

The basic **Pbv 302** interior may also be configured as a front line load carrier for 2 tonnes of stores, or as an armoured ambulance.

Projects to produce 'product improved' versions of the **Pbv 302** came to nothing. Developments of the basic **Pbv 302** chassis, also from Hagglunds, include an armoured bridgelayer (Brobv 941) and an armoured recovery vehicle (Bgbv 82), both using hulls similar to that of the **Pbv 302**.

The Ikv-91 tank destroyer is also based on a chassis essentially similar to that of the **Pbv 302.**

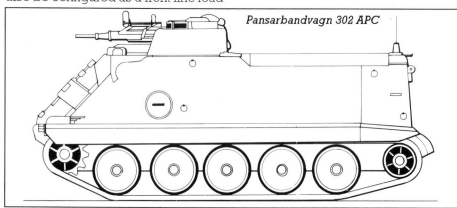

Pansarbandvagn 302 APC

Specification

Crew: 2
Seating: 10
Weight: (combat) 13,500 kg
Length: 5.35 m
Width: 2.86 m
Height: (hull top) 1.9 m
Ground clearance: 0.4 m
Track: 2.42 m
Max speed: (road) 66 km/h
Fuel capacity: 285 litres
Range: 300 km
Fording: amphibious
Vertical obstacle: 0.6 m
Engine: Volvo-Penta Model THD 100B diesel
Power output: 280 hp
Suspension: torsion bar
Armament: 1 x 20 mm cannon
Variants: See text

The Swedish Pbv 302 APC, one of the first APCs to be armed with a 20 mm cannon as standard.

MOWAG Piranha   Switzerland

The **MOWAG Piranha** is perhaps the most diverse of all vehicles in the wheeled APC/IFV category for not only is it produced in 4 x 4, 6 x 6, 8 x 8 and 10 x 10 forms but it is also licence-produced in at least three countries and has been manufactured to suit a whole host of armoured vehicles roles and requirements.

Close derivatives such as the Light Armored Vehicle (LAV - qv) and Canadian Bison (qv) are based directly on the **MOWAG Piranha** which was originally developed as a private venture in Switzerland during the early 1970s. Since then the type has sold widely to about 11 countries with sales from some of the licence-producers (Canada (General Motors), Chile (FAMAE) and the United Kingdom (GKN Defence)) adding to that total.

The Swiss Army purchased 6 x 6 and 8 x 8 examples, as have many others, although to date the 4 x 4 models have had only relatively limited sales success.

All configurations follow a common outline and there are many components shared by all models. The well-shaped steel hull has the engine well forward next to the driver while the main troop compartment is to the rear.

A wide variety of turrets or external weapon stations, including some for ATGWs, can be installed centrally on the hull roof.

The larger models can mount gun turrets with up to 90 mm guns while the 10 x 10 model, first seen in 1994, can accommodate a 105 mm tank gun turret. The 8 x 8 models can also accommodate a 105 mm gun turret, with one model having a 120 mm breech-loaded mortar in a traversing turret (most models can carry 81 or 120 mm mortars internally).

Lighter models can tow 120 mm mortars or air defence missile system trailers such as those for the British Aerospace Jernas system. There are also recovery vehicle models, command posts, internal security (IS) and multiple rocket launchers (MRL).

Well over 2,700 Piranhas of all types have been manufactured in Switzerland alone.

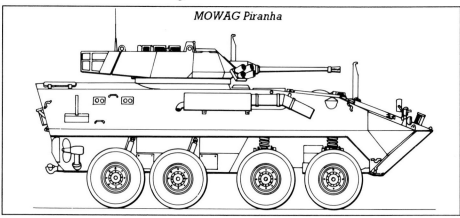

MOWAG Piranha

Specification

(6 x 6)
Crew: 2
Seating: up to 12
Weight: (combat) 10,500 kg
Length: 5.97 m
Width: 2.5 m
Height: 1.85 m
Ground clearance: 0.5 m
Track: 2.2 m
Max speed: (road) 100 km/h
Fuel capacity: 200 litres
Range: 600 km
Fording: amphibious
Vertical obstacle: 0.5 m
Engine: Detroit Diesel 6V-53T diesel
Power output: 300 hp
Suspension: independent
Armament: See text
Variants: Many, see text

An 8 x 8 model of the Piranha APC armed with an externally mounted 12.7 mm MG.

Warrior MCV

The tracked IFV known to the British Army as the **Warrior** was originally known as MCV-80. Intended to replace the old FV432 APC, the vehicles was developed via a series of pre-production prototypes from 1980 onwards, with production by GKN Defence commencing during 1986.

The **Warrior** has been in British Army service since 1988, seeing combat in the Gulf in 1991. The original order was for over 1,000 units but Army reorganisations reduced that to 789 of all types, sufficient to equip seven Mechanised Infantry battalions.

The base model is the Warrior Section Vehicle armed with a 30 mm RARDEN cannon and a 7.62 mm Chain Gun in a two-man turret. The seven troops carried enter through a door in the hull rear; once they are inside there are sufficient combat supplies carried to maintain them in action for at least 48 hours.

Vehicles in the Gulf were provided with extra passive armour panels but these are not normally carried during peacetime operations.

The British Army also operates a Warrior Mechanised Artillery Observation Vehicle (MAOV) on which the only turret armament is a 7.62 mm Chain Gun and a dummy cannon barrel. There are two repair and recovery vehicles, the Warrior Mechanised Recovery Vehicle (Repair) (MCV(R)) and Mechanised Combat Repair Vehicle (MCRV), both armed with a single 7.62 mm Chain Gun and equipped for their roles with winches, cranes and other equipment.

A Warrior Command Vehicle is produced in four sub-variants (one for the artillery), all outwardly identical to the Section Vehicle.

Warriors may be fitted with dozer blades or light mine-clearing ploughs and an ATGW Warrior carrying MILAN or (eventually) TRIGAT is entering service.

Several trial armament installations have been tested on **Warrior** including one with a 90 mm gun turret.

A special hot weather version known as Desert Warrior, or Fahris, has been ordered by Kuwait - this model has a 25 mm cannon main armament.

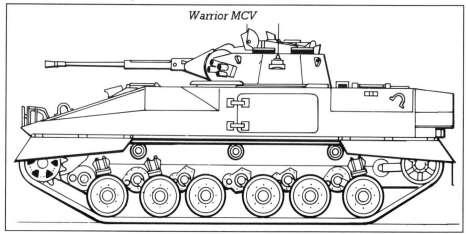

Warrior MCV

Specification

(Section Vehicle, fully armoured)
Crew: 3
Seating: 7
Weight: (combat) 25,700 kg
Length: 6.34 m
Width: 3.034 m
Height: (hull top) 1.93 m
Ground clearance: 0.49 m
Track: approx 2.6 m
Max speed: (road) 75 km/h
Fuel capacity: 770 litres
Range: 660 km
Fording: 1.3 m
Vertical obstacle: 0.75 m
Engine: Perkins CV-8 TCA diesel
Power output: 550 hp
Suspension: torsion bar
Armament: 1 x 30 mm cannon;
1 x 7.62 mm Chain Gun
Variants: Many, see text

A Warrior IFV lacking the 'full combat' additional side armour as used in The Gulf.

Warrior (cont.)

Right: Rear view of Warrior with turret slewed rearwards, revealing infantry access hatch.

Below: Mud-spattered Warrior with all hatches open, showing the driver's periscope.

Opposite: Diagrammatic view of standard section-vehicle seating arrangement.

Inset: Diagrammatic view of the Desert Fighting Vehicle seating configuration.

FV103 Spartan APC

The **FV103 Spartan** tracked APC was not developed in isolation but as part of an armoured combat vehicle family headed by the Scorpion light reconnaissance vehicle armed with a 76 mm gun. There are seven main members in the family, all produced by Alvis Vehicles, in which the **Spartan** was intended to be a specialist combat team carrier. This means that the **Spartan** is not normally operated as an infantry combat section vehicle but as a combat engineer, battlefield reconnaissance or air defence missile team carrier.

Since the British Army has reorganised, many **Spartans** have become available from their former employment so are now widely issued as general purpose liaison and patrol vehicles. The chassis and suspension of the **Spartan** are shared with all other members of the Scorpion family, as is the Jaguar petrol engine but on the **Spartan** the aluminium hull is enlarged to a box configuration to accommodate the driver, team commander/radio operator and the vehicle commander who also operates the 7.62 mm MG mounted over his cupola; the MG can be aimed and fired from within the vehicle.

The troop compartment at the rear seats four personnel with space for their specialised and personal equipment; more equipment can be stowed externally in racks or boxes. Some **Spartans** have provision for mounting a battlefield surveillance radar on the hull roof while others have internal racking for air defence missiles. At one time the British Infantry had tank destroyer **Spartans** with MILAN ATGW launcher turrets on their roof but these have now been withdrawn. Another variant was known as the Streaker (mainly due to its high speed potential although all members of the Scorpion family are agile and fast). The Streaker was a **Spartan** chassis with an open flat bed rear to act as a front line stores transporter or mine dispensing equipment carrier - it did not pass the prototype stage.

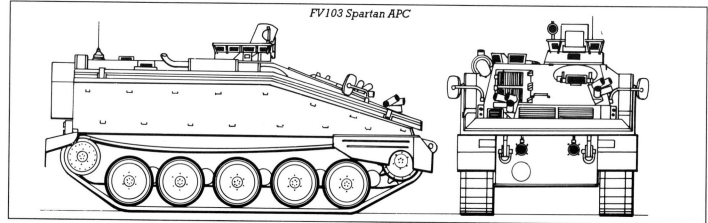

FV103 Spartan APC

Specification

Crew: 3
Seating: 4
Weight: (combat) 8,172 kg
Length: 5.125 m
Width: 2.134 m
Height: 2.26 m
Ground clearance: 0.356 m
Track: 1.708 m
Max speed: (road) 80.5 km/h
Fuel capacity: 386 litres
Range: 483 km
Fording: 1.067 m
Vertical obstacle: 0.5 m
Engine: Jaguar J60 No 1 Mk 100B petrol
Power output: 190 hp
Suspension: torsion bar
Armament: 1 x 7.62 mm MG
Variants: None, see text

A Spartan APC as once used by the RAF Regiment but now phased out to other duties.

Stormer APC

The **Stormer** tracked APC was originally developed by the British Ministry of Defence and first shown, as the FV4333, in 1978. It was intended to be a general purpose APC or combat vehicle platform created by extending the overall length of the Spartan chassis (see previous entry) and adding an extra road wheel station each side; engine, transmission and suspension changes were also incorporated. This virtually doubled the carrying capacity of the Spartan and provided a much more versatile platform for further development.

The prototypes, armed with a 7.62 mm MG over the commander's position, underwent much testing and trials before the manufacturing and marketing rights were acquired by Alvis Vehicles. Further development ensued but the **Stormer** has yet to be employed operationally as an APC. Instead the extended armoured box hull model has been acquired fitted out as a command vehicle by Oman to support their Chieftain 2 MBTs.

The British Army has procured **Stormers** in a modified form to act as the mobile platform for the Shorts Starstreak high velocity missile (HVM), the first of 151 systems originally ordered entering service from 1995 onwards. On this variant, which has a three-man crew, the Starstreak launchers are located towards the rear together with their target sensors. Reload missiles are carried inside the hull. (A similar arrangement has been proposed for the Shorts Starburst air defence missile system.).

A future **Stormer** application may be that of flat bed carrier for the British Army's scatterable mine system, once it has been selected; a Giat Minotaur mine dispensing system and **Stormer** flat bed combination was taken to the Gulf in 1990/1991 but not tested operationally.

Other proposed roles for the basic **Stormer** are many, including an IFV with a cannon-armed turret on the roof; several trials installations have been made.

Another trial vehicle was configured as a forward artillery observation vehicle, equipped with suitable sensors and communications equipment.

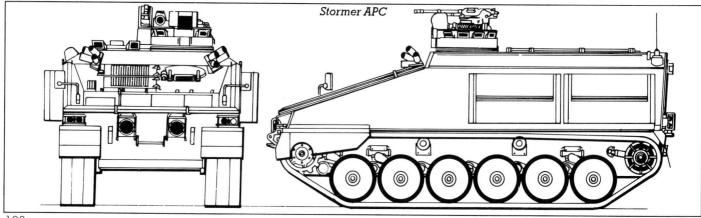

Stormer APC

Specification

Crew: 3
Seating: 8
Weight: (combat, max) 12,700 kg
Length: 5.33 m
Width: 2.4 m
Height: 2.27 m
Ground clearance: 0.425 m
Track: 1.892 m
Max speed: (road) 80 km/h
Fuel capacity: 405 litres
Range: 650 km
Fording: 1.1 m
Vertical obstacle: 0.6 m
Engine: Perkins T6.3544 diesel
Power output: 250 hp
Suspension: torsion bar
Armament: See text
Variants: Starstreak HVM - see also text

A Stormer APC configured as the carrier for the Starstreak air defence missile system.

Saxon APC

The **Saxon** wheeled APC was developed by GKN Defence to provide a relatively low cost APC based on a revised Bedford 4 x 4 truck chassis and other commercially available components such as the engine and transmission. Developed from the earlier and less protected AT104, the base model was the AT105 which later became the **Saxon** before being ordered by the British Army in 1983 to provide United Kingdom-based infantry battalions to travel to North-West Europe in an emergency and still retain a measure of operational protection and mobility once arrived.

The **Saxon** is thus basically an armoured truck with limited cross country mobility but still capable of operating in forward areas.

The hull is welded steel with V-shaped under-chassis plates to deflect mine detonations. Seating is provided in the rear for up to ten troops, although eight is a more comfortable load if all their equipment is included - there is an equipment stowage area on the hull roof. Two doors are provided, one each side, plus another at the rear. The commander has a fixed cupola over which a 7.62 mm MG can be mounted on an unprotected pintle, although some **Saxons** operating in the former Yugoslavia were modified by the Army to accommodate small one-man MG turrets taken from old FV432 APCs.

British Army **Saxon** variants include a recovery vehicle with a side-mounted winch, and a command vehicle, some of which are operated by Royal Artillery air defence regiments. Special **Saxons** procured for operations in Northern Ireland include the **Saxon** Patrol with a Cummins 160 hp diesel engine and special internal security (IS) equipment such as a barricade removal device and spotlights; there is also a Northern Ireland armoured ambulance.

Other **Saxon** variants, some of which have been exported to nations such as Hong Kong, Oman, Malaysia and Nigeria, are usually configured as IS vehicles.

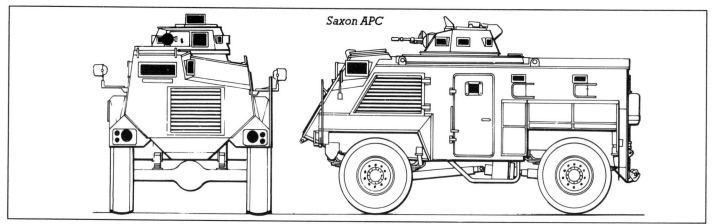

Saxon APC

Specification

Crew: 2
Seating: up to 10
Weight: (combat) up to 11,200 kg
Length: 5.35 m
Width: 2.5 m
Height: 2.19 m
Ground clearance: 0.33 m
Track: 2.06 m
Max speed: (road) 100 km/h
Fuel capacity: 296 litres
Range: 660 km
Fording: 1 m
Vertical obstacle: 0.45 m
Engine: Perkins 210 Ti diesel
Power output: 210 hp
Suspension: leaf spring
Armament: 1 x 7.62 mm MG
Variants: See text

The Saxon wheeled APC, demonstrating its origins as an armoured truck.

Simba APC

The **Simba** has many automotive features in common with the Saxon APC (see previous entry) but was designed for what are described as light combat vehicle or low profile internal security (IS) roles. Developed by GKN Defence as a private venture with a view to local manufacture in less developed countries, the basic 4 x 4 **Simba** can be readily configured to suit many military and para-military functions, from an APC to a fire support vehicle mounting a 90 mm gun in a turret; the latter has been trialled.

To date the most important **Simba** model has been that selected by the

Armed Forces of the Philippines who have ordered 150 units, most for local assembly using, at first, knock-down kits supplied by GKN. These vehicles, most of which are general purpose APCs likely to be operated in IS situations, have an armoured steel hull surmounted by a 12.7 mm MG in a one man turret; single or twin 7.62 mm MGs are options.

Troops enter and leave the vehicle via a single large door in the hull rear; the driver has his own roof hatch and is protected by bullet-proof screens. Up to ten troops can be carried but a more comfortable load is eight; a fully dedicated APC could seat up to 12 troops. The hull

can be converted to carry a turntable-mounted 81 mm mortar firing through open roof hatches, while a TOW or HOT ATGW launcher turret could be located on the roof.

An IFV variant with a 20 or 25 mm turret has also been proposed. However, the most likely **Simba** variant is an IS vehicle fitted with a barricade removal device, a turret-mounted anti-riot agent projectors, a riot agent filtration system for the vehicle occupants, side-mounted riot screens, and loudspeakers.

Optional equipment for all models includes air conditioning and a winch.

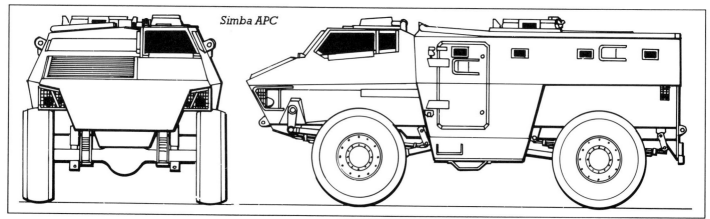

Simba APC

Specification

Crew: 2
Seating: up to 10
Weight: (combat) up to 11,200 kg
Length: 5.35 m
Width: 2.5 m
Height: 2.19 m
Ground clearance: 0.33 m
Track: 2.06 m
Max speed: (road) 100 km/h
Fuel capacity: 296 litres
Range: 660 km
Fording: 1 m
Vertical obstacle: 0.45 m
Engine: Perkins 210 Ti diesel
Power output: 210 hp
Suspension: leaf spring
Armament: 1 x 12.7 mm MG
Variants: See text

The Simba APC is seen here in its role as an internal security vehicle.

Shorland S 55 APC

The **Shorland S 55** APC is the latest in a line of wheeled APCs dating back to 1973, all produced by Short Brothers and utilising the basic chassis and automotive components of the long-established Land Rover.

The **Shorland S 55** is based on the chassis of the Land Rover Defender 110, allied to an armoured body which closely follows the outlines of the Land Rover original to the extent that some 85 per cent of the automotive components are commercially available Land Rover parts. Power steering is provided and the suspension is modified to cater for the increased weights involved.

Intended primarily as an internal security (IS) vehicle for police and para-military units, the **Shorland S 55** is also employed operationally by military forces and has been exported to over 20 countries, some of whom utilise Shorlands for long range or road patrols in disputed areas.

The armour provides protection against 7.62 mm AP projectiles while the glass-reinforced underside is proof against most land mines.

For extra protection the roof and bonnet areas are ridged to allow petrol bombs to roll off. All windscreens and side windows are bullet resistant while the six occupants in the rear are provided with small vision blocks and firing ports.

The driver and commander enter through armoured side doors; the troop compartment has a two-piece rear door.

On some Shorlands the roof hatch over the commander can be used to mount a 7.62 mm MG.

Smoke dischargers are often standard and some vehicles have provision for riot agent projectors. Fire retardant internal trim is provided on most models while a spare wheel is often carried on the roof.

Other vehicles in the **Shorland** range include the S 52 armoured car, the S 53 air defence vehicle, and the S 54, described as an anti-hijack vehicle.

If required a 107 hp diesel engine can be fitted in place of the usual Land Rover V-8 petrol unit.

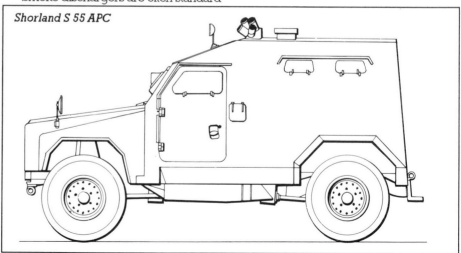

Shorland S 55 APC

Specification

Crew: 2
Seating: 6
Weight: (combat) 3,600 kg
Length: 4.25 m
Width: 1.8 m
Height: 2.28 m
Ground clearance: 0.324 m
Track: 1.5 m
Max speed: (road) 120 km/h
Fuel capacity: 136 litres
Range: over 630 km
Fording: not known
Vertical obstacle: 0.23 m
Engine: Land Rover 3.5-litre V-8 petrol
Power output: 134 hp
Suspension: coil spring
Armament: See text
Variants: S 52, S 53, S 54

A Shorland wheeled APC in 'civvie' guise as an armoured carrier for CNN television crews operating in Bosnia.

Bradley M2 IFV

In 1972 the US Army requested design proposals to meet a requirement for a mechanised infantry fighting vehicle (MIFV). A complex series of design submissions and changing specifications followed until a Fighting Vehicle System (FVS) appeared, comprising two vehicles, an IFV which became the **M2 Bradley**, and a Cavalry Fighting Vehicle which became the M3 CFV. Deliveries by FMC (now United Defense) commenced in 1981 and have continued since with totals approaching the 8,000 plus the US Army has requested - procurement plans until 2008 have been made.

The **M2 Bradley** IFV is based around a welded aluminium hull and is armed with a two-man turret with a 25 mm Chain Gun and two TOW ATGW launchers - there is also a 7.62 mm coaxial MG. Reactive armour panels for added protection can be added to late production (M2A2 and M2A3) examples, while early models had firing ports with dedicated rifles attached - these were later removed to avoid compromising the side armour protection. Throughout its service life the **M2 Bradley** IFV series has been the subject of numerous enhancements to improve combat capabilities and

survivability for the vehicle and occupants so, apart from the reactive armour panels, extras such as improved armour, automotive improvements, strengthened suspension components, etc, have been added and more such improvements are planned.

The **M3** CFV carries only two extra troops in addition to the three-man crew as it is intended to be a scouting vehicle, whereas the **M2** IFV has provision for six.

The **M2** and **M3** are amphibious and

air-transportable, with the swimming capabilities improved by the erection of inflatable buoyancy tanks.

Numerous derivatives, mainly based on the **M2** IFV, have been produced, including air defence missile carriers, while the basic chassis has been adapted for other purposes, such as the (much modified) chassis for the Multiple Launch Rocket System (MLRS).

Some 400 **M2** IFVs have been exported to Saudi Arabia.

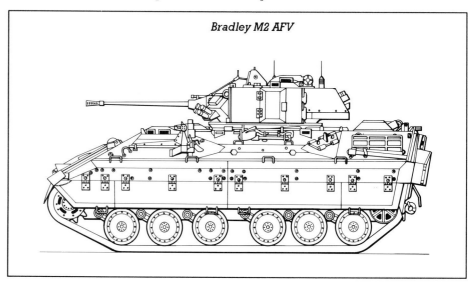

Bradley M2 AFV

Specifications:

Crew: 3
Seating: 6
Weight: (combat) 22,590 kg
Length: 6.453 m
Width: 3.2 m
Height: 2.565 m
Ground clearance: 0.432 m
Track: approx 2.35 m
Max speed: (road) 66 km/h
Fuel capacity: 662 litres
Range: 66 km
Fording: amphibious

Vertical obstacle: 0.9 m
Engine: Cummins VTA-903T diesel
Power output: 500 hp
Suspension: torsion bar
Armament: 1 x 25 mm cannon;
1 x 7.62 mm MG;
1 x 2-tube TOW ATGW launcher
Variants: M3 CFV - also see text

*An M2 Bradley IFV at speed during
acceptance trials.*

FMC Armored IFV   USA

The **Armored Infantry Fighting Vehicle (AIFV)** grew out of a project to provide the M113 APC (see following entry) with an enclosed weapon station. Private venture development by FMC (now United Defense) resulted, in 1970, in the **AIFV** which was first procured by the Netherlands. Their original order was for over 2,000 **AIFV**s, about half of which were manufactured in the Netherlands. Other customers have included Belgium and Turkey, both of whom undertook local licence production agreements. Production in Belgium has now ceased but it continues in Turkey where the local requirement is for some 1,700 **AIFV**s.

The **AIFV** is basically an M113 APC with a revised hull outline and a turret off-set to the right, just behind the engine compartment, and mounting a 25 mm cannon with a coaxial 7.62 mm MG.

Many **AIFV**s are armed with a TOW ATGW turret, especially those produced in the Netherlands, where another model is armed only with an 12.7 mm MG over a small cupola. The addition of the turret limits the internal troop accommodation to a maximum of seven who enter via a power-operated ramp at the rear.

Customers, other than those already mentioned, have included the Philippines (where the turret armament is limited to a 12.7 mm MG) and Egypt, the latter purchasing surplus vehicles from the Netherlands.

At one time Pakistan was to produce the **AIFV** locally but that arrangement is in abeyance. With so many **AIFV**s being produced at several centres, variants have proliferated to the extent that, for example, Belgian and Netherlands command **AIFV**s differ. Thus there are several types of **AIFV** recovery vehicle, armoured ambulance, and so on. There are also **AIFV** supply vehicles, and mortar carriers or tractors.

Some Turkish **AIFV**s are fitted with 300 hp diesel engine packs.

A close copy of the **AIFV** has been produced in Taiwan. The Korean Infantry Fighting Vehicle (qv) is visually similar to the **AIFV**.

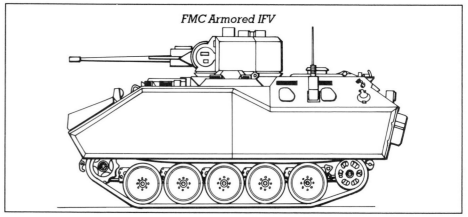

FMC Armored IFV

Specification

Crew: 3
Seating: 7
Weight: (combat) 13.687 kg
Length: 5.258 m
Width: 2.819 m
Height: (hull top) 1.854 m
Ground clearance: 0.432 m
Track: approx 2.2 m
Max speed: (road) 61 km/h
Fuel capacity: 416 litres
Range: 490 km
Fording: amphibious
Vertical obstacle: 0.635 m
Engine: Detroit Diesel 6V-53T V-6 diesel
Power output: 264 hp
Suspension: torsion bar
Armament: 1 x 25 mm cannon;
1 x 7.62 mm MG
Variants: See text

The FMC Armoured Infantry Fighting Vehicle (AIFV), produced in several forms in various countries.

M113 APC

When mentioning the **M113** series of APCs it is difficult to avoid superlatives, for the type has become the most widely-produced and utilised APC of the Western World. Since production by FMC (now United Defense) commenced in 1960 well over 32,000 **M113**s and its derivatives have been received by the US Army alone and the overall production total in 1992 had reached nearly 75,000 of all types; production seems set to continue both in the USA and with several licence-producers elsewhere.

Yet despite the huge number of variants and sub-variants, the base **M113** APC remains a welded aluminium box-shaped hull set on an uncomplicated tracked chassis.

Over the years the size and weight of the vehicle has grown and numerous components have been altered to accommodate that growth but the basic outline has remained the same - the latest production model is the **M113A3** with a longer hull, more armour, a more powerful engine, and a revised layout of items such as the fuel cells which are moved to the hull rear, either side of the main entry ramp.

On nearly all models the main armament has been a single 12.7 mm MG on a pintle over the commander's cupola; sometimes this station is set behind a shield or small open turret but variations abound, as indeed they do for the entire **M113** series.

Derivatives are legion, ranging from command posts (M577) to anti-tank vehicles armed with TOW ATGW turrets (M901). There are also mortar carriers (M125 for 81 mm, M1064 for 120 mm), smoke screen producing vehicles (M1059), numerous air defence missile and gun carriers, combat engineer vehicles, ambulances, recovery and repair vehicles, etc.

Many user nations have added their own variations and modifications, as have licence producers such as Belgium and Italy. The list could continue but would fill this book.

M113s and variants are used by at least 48 countries.

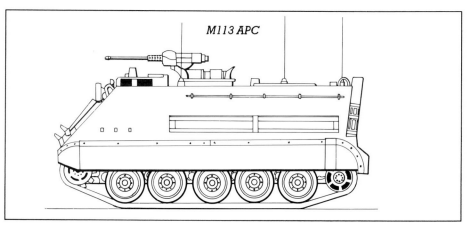

M113 APC

Specification

(M113A3)
Crew: 2
Seating: 11
Weight: (combat) 12,150 kg
Length: 5.3 m
Width: 2.686 m
Height: (hull top) 1.85 m
Ground clearance: 0.43 m
Track: 2.159 m
Max speed: (road) 66 km/h
Fuel capacity: 360 litres
Range: 480 km
Fording: amphibious
Vertical obstacle: 0.61 m
Engine: Detroit Diesel 6V-53T V-6 diesel
Power output: 275 hp
Suspension: torsion bar
Armament: 1 x 12.7 mm MG
Variants: Many - see text

An Australian Army M113 APC, one of the many users of the most ubiquitous APC in the West.

AAV7A1 Amphibious APC

USA

The **Amphibious Assault Vehicle 7A1**, usually now known as the **AAV7A1**, was once called the LVTP7A1 by the US Marine Corps and other users. It is a bulky amphibious tracked vehicle intended to land troops on open beaches so it has to be seaworthy and is thus scaled accordingly.

Intended as a replacement for the LVTP5 series (see following entry) the first AAV7 (then the LVTP7) prototype appeared in 1967 with production commencing during 1970-71. By the time production had ceased over 1,500 had been produced. not only for the US Marines but also for seven export customers.

The late production model was the **AAV7A1** and most earlier models were later brought up to this standard. **AAV7A1** improvements included a new Cummins diesel engine pack, night vision devices, a new weapon station control system, improved ventilation and many other detail changes. Further improvements are scheduled, including a universal weapon mounting capable of accommodating a 40 mm grenade launcher as well as MGs. The main armament carried on current **AAV7A1s** is a 12.7 mm MG in a small turret on the right-hand side of the engine installation; the driver and commander are seated to the left of the engine.

The capacious troop compartment can hold up to 25 marines or 4.5 tonnes of supplies, with entry and exit being via a large rear-mounted ramp.

In the water, propulsion is provided by two water jet units at the rear. A kit was devised to permit extra applique armour panels to be installed on most US Marine Corps vehicles.

AAV7A1 variants include a command vehicle, a recovery vehicle fitted with a recovery jib, and various mine-clearing vehicles, including one with a mine plough.

Various automotive and suspension test beds have appeared, including a project involving an electric drive system. In time it is expected that the **AAV7A1** will be replaced by a programme known as the Advanced Amphibious Assault Vehicle.

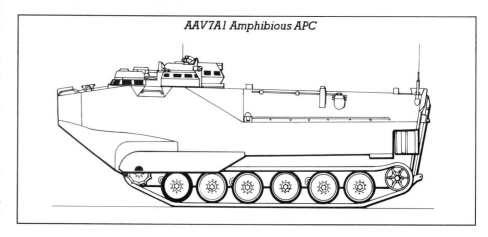

AAV7A1 Amphibious APC

Specification

Crew: 3
Seating: 25
Weight: (combat) 23,990 kg
Length: 7.943 m
Width: 3.27 m
Height: 3.263 m
Ground clearance: 0.406 m
Track: 2.61 m
Max speed: (road) 72.4 km/h
Fuel capacity: 647 litres
Range: 482 km
Fording: amphibious
Vertical obstacle: 0.9 m
Engine: Cummins VT400 diesel
Power output: 400 hp
Suspension: torsion bar
Armament: 1 x 12.7 mm MG
Variants: See text

The amphibious AAV7 APC used by the US Marine Corps and others.

LVTP5A1 Amphibious APC   USA

The **Landing Vehicle, Tracked, Personnel 5A1**, or **LVTP5A1**, dates from the early 1950s. It has been out of service with its original users, the US Marine Corps, since the mid-1970s, having been replaced by the LVTP7/AAV7 (see previous entry). The type still soldiers on with nations such as Chile, the Philippines and Taiwan, the latter still operating a fleet of over 350 **LVTP5A1** vehicles by some accounts.

The **LVTP5A1** was a successor to the US Marines' amphibious assault vehicles from World War 2 era and is thus a bulky armoured steel box on a tracked chassis, powered by a fuel-thirsty V-12 petrol engine. The main troop compartment, or hold, has seating for up to 34 Marines; up to 45 standing personnel could be carried as an emergency measure. With the seating removed there is capacity to carry up to 5.4 tonnes of combat supplies for floating operations (over 8 tonnes when on land), a towed 105 mm howitzer and some ammunition, or small Jeep-

type vehicles, all of which may be loaded through a large roof hatch. Once in the water the **LVTP5A1** is propelled by its tracks which have special water grousers to aid propulsion.

The usual armament carried is a 7.62 mm MG over a roof hatch, although there was a fire support model known as the LVTH6 with a two-man turret mounting a short-barrelled 105 mm howitzer.

Other variants included a command

vehicle converted from the APC, a recovery vehicle, and a combat engineer model with a front-mounted dozer blade. A kit could convert the APC into an ambulance. How many of these variants remain in service is not known.

The Taiwanese have carried out their own update modifications to their **LVTP5A1** fleet, including the replacement of the petrol engine by more fuel-efficient 750 hp diesel packs and the installation of a revised fuel system.

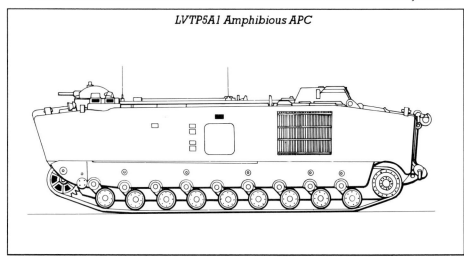

LVTP5A1 Amphibious APC

Specification:

Crew: 3
Seating: 34
Weight: (combat) 30,144 kg
Length: 9.042 m
Width: 3.567 m
Height: (hull top) 2.565 m
Ground clearance: 0.457 m
Track: approx 2.97 m
Max speed: (road) 48 km/h
Fuel capacity: 1,726 litres
Range: 306 km
Fording: amphibious
Vertical obstacle: 0.9 m
Engine: Continental LV-1790-1 V-12 petrol
Power output: 810 hp
Suspension: torsilastic
Armament: 1 x 7.62 mm MG
Variants: See text

Despite its design age the LVTP-5 amphibious APC is still operated by Taiwan and others.

139

Dragoon APC

USA

The **Dragoon** wheeled APC is a product of the AV Technology Corporation and is based on the experience gained from the production and marketing of earlier vehicles, also under the **Dragoon** label.

The **Dragoon** is not a single vehicle but a family of wheeled armoured vehicles intended to meet most military and para-military requirements. All members of the family are based on an armoured steel monocoque hull with two side doors; the engine pack is at the rear. Most of the automotive and other components are based on commercially available or in-service military parts available world-wide.

The **Dragoon** is fully amphibious. Inside the hull there is seating for 11 occupants, plus the driver, with a roof hatch located behind the driver's position. A 12.7 mm MG can be ring- or pintle-mounted over this roof hatch, although other weapons could be installed to allow the **Dragoon** APC to be used as a patrol or reconnaissance vehicle.

If required, the **Dragoon** APC can be provided with a MG or 40 mm grenade launcher turret, one version known as the Dragoon Light Forces Vehicle mounting a 90 mm gun and a coaxial MG (LFV-90 mm), although the crew of this model is limited to four.

The basic APC can be configured as an 81 mm mortar carrier with the mortar firing through side-opening roof hatches. The hull could also be used to accommodate communications or electronic warfare (EW) suites and a 1-tonne payload logistics carrier with a self-loading crane is available.

An armoured security vehicle (ASV) model known as the Dragoon Patroller, some with raised and extended cabs, has been procured by various American police forces, and a tank-destroyer ATGW carrier armed with TOW missiles has been proposed.

The US Army and Navy have obtained some **Dragoon** vehicles, as have Thailand and Canada.

The largest customer to date has been Venezuela who ordered 100 units.

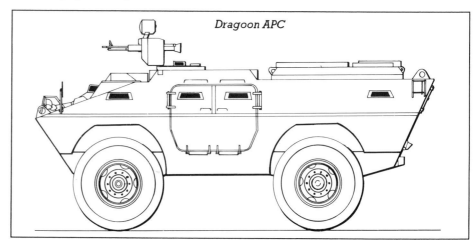

Dragoon APC

Specification

Crew: 2
Seating: 10
Weight: (combat) 13,068 kg
Length: 5.89 m
Width: 2.49 m
Height: (hull top) 2.08 m
Ground clearance: 0.38 m
Track: 1.98 m
Max speed: (road) 116 km/h
Fuel capacity: 350 litres
Range: 885 km
Fording: amphibious
Vertical obstacle: 0.61 m
Engine: Detroit Diesel 6V-53T diesel
Power output: 300 hp
Suspension: elliptical springs
Armament: 1 x 12.7 mm MG
Variants: See text

Frontal view of a turret-armed Dragoon wheeled APC.

Cadillac Gage LAV-150 ST

USA

The **Cadillac-Gage LAV-150** series of wheeled APCs has been established since 1963 when the prototype of a vehicle then known as the V-100 Commando was rolled out. The 4 x 4 V-100 was acquired by the US armed forces for a variety of functions, from air base security to route patrolling in Vietnam; many of the V-100 models remain in widespread service.

From those vehicles came the V-200 with a more powerful engine and, eventually, the LAV-300 with a 6 x 6 drive configuration. Then came the V-150 series, later renamed the **LAV-150** The current production version is the **LAV-150** ST which denotes stretched and turbocharger, resulting in increased internal capacity and better all-round automotive performance, especially as the original petrol engine was replaced by a diesel unit.

In general appearance the **LAV-150** series usually resemble light armoured cars for most have a two-man turret armed with a 20 mm cannon plus an optional coaxial 7.62 mm MG; some APC examples lack the turret and have

a pintle-mounted 12.7 mm MG in its place.

The hull can accommodate up to seven troops although on many models this is limited to five. However, over the years the **LAV-150** and its associated models have been produced in many alternative forms for export to about 24 countries; Saudi Arabia alone took over 1,100 units.

Production, now by Textron Marine & Land Systems, stands at around 3,000 of all types. These types range from 76 or 90 mm gun carriers with turrets (neither of which has apparently reached

production), to recovery and air defence vehicles with 20 mm rotary cannon.

Other models include the usual command, internal security (IS), and mortar carrier variants; a TOW ATGW carrier has been proposed. A turretless base security model is operated by the US Air Force.

Turkey ordered over 120 units, some of them configured for the police emergency rescue vehicle role.

Other significant **LAV-150** users include Indonesia, the Philippines, Singapore, Thailand, Taiwan, Venezuela and Malaysia.

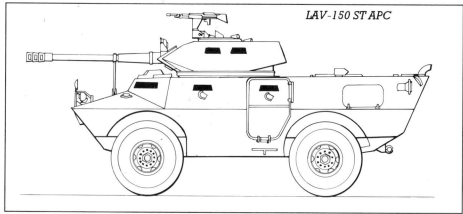

LAV-150 ST APC

Specification

(LAV-150 ST)
Crew: 2
Seating: 7
Weight: (combat) 10,886 kg
Length: 6.274 m
Width: 2.39 m
Height: (hull roof) 1.98 m
Ground clearance: 0.381 m
Track: 1.98 m
Max speed: (road) 112 km/h
Fuel capacity: 303 litres
Range: 800 km
Fording: amphibious
Vertical obstacle: 0.61 m
Engine: 6 CTA diesel
Power output: 250 hp
Suspension: leaf springs and shock absorbers
Armament: 1 x 20 mm cannon; 2 x 7.62 mm MG
Variants: See text

A 4 x 4 model of the Commando wheeled APC.

Glossary

AAAV	Advanced amphibious assault vehicle
AAV	Anti-aircraft vehicle **or**
AAV	Amphibious assault vehicle
ACV	Airborne combat vehicle
AEV	Armoured engineering vehicle
AIFV	Armored infantry fighting vehicle
APC	Armoured personnel carrier
APFSDS	Armour piercing fin stablised discarding sabot
ARV	Armoured recovery vehicle
ASV	Armored security vehicle
ATGW	Anti-tank guided weapon
CFV	Cavalry fighting vehicle
CIS	Commonwealth of Independent States
EAOS	Enhanced artillery observation system
EW	Electronic warfare
FCV	Forward command vehicle
FMC	Food Machinery Corporation
FOV	Forward observation vehicle
FRAG-HE	Fragmenting high explosive
FV	Field vehicle
FVS	Fighting vehicle system
HE	High explosive
HVM	High velocity missile
ICV	Infantry combat vehicle
IFV	Infantry fighting vehicle
IS	Internal security
KIFV	Korean infantry fighting vehicle
LAV	Light armored vehicle
LFV	Light forces vehicle
LVTP	Landing vehicle, tracked, personnel
MAOV	Mechanised artillery observation vehicle
MBT	Main battle tank
MC	Mortar carrier
MCRV	Mechanised combat repair vehicle
MCV	Mechanised combat vehicle
MG	Machine gun
MICV	Mechanised infantry combat vehicle
MLRS	Multiple launch rocket system
MRL	Multiple rocket launcher
MRV(R)	Mechanised recovery vehicle (repair)
NBC	Nuclear, biological and chemical